COASTAL
South Carolina
Fish & Game

COASTAL
South Carolina
Fish & Game

HISTORY, CULTURE AND CONSERVATION

JAMES O. LUKEN

THE
History
PRESS

Published by The History Press
Charleston, SC
www.historypress.com

Copyright © 2021 by James O. Luken
All rights reserved

First published 2021

Manufactured in the United States

ISBN 9781467146821

Library of Congress Control Number: 2020951648

Contents

Acknowledgements

I was inspired to write this book after perusing the historical images in Lee Brockington's *Plantation Between the Waters: A Brief History of Hobcaw Barony.* Some of these photographs depicted catches of fish and harvests of game not currently possible or allowed. An expanded search of images in the Georgetown County Library also provided glimpses of a historical coastal fish and game landscape characterized by larger sizes and bigger numbers relative to the present. These preserved and digitized images provided a springboard for considering the broader environmental and regulatory changes that have occurred on the coast of South Carolina.

Libraries that digitize and then make available historical photographs are actively participating in an important process of understanding historical ecology. I am particularly grateful to Julie Warren at the Georgetown County Library, Grace Cordial at the Beaufort County Library and Lee Brockington at the Belle W. Baruch Foundation for accessing certain photographs and then granting permission to use them. Beth Bilderback of the South Caroliniana Library and Leah Michelle Worthington at the College of Charleston Library also helped to locate and then make available materials from their collections. These efforts were made more difficult than normal by the work conditions imposed by COVID-19, and I thank everyone for their help.

Phil Wilkinson graciously provided scans of his personal collection of duck stamps and gave some insight into historical hunting practices in coastal South Carolina. William Shaw of Remington Arms Company dug into a collection of historical advertisements and helped locate the best ones. I made regular use of digital photos posted by the U.S. Fish and Wildlife Service, the National Archives and the Library of Congress. Their efforts here are commendable in terms of making high-quality photographs available for public viewing.

Ben Burroughs of the Horry County Archives Center gave me some important guidance on digitizing historical photographs, and Derek Crane in the Department of Biology at CCU helped identify fishes in blurry photographs. Finally, Anne Monk read the entire manuscript and made numerous valuable suggestions for improvement. Her interest in this project was very much appreciated.

Introduction

A straight line tracing the South Carolina coast measures only 187 miles. But these miles are not like the miles farther inland, where travel is easy and scenery lackluster. These coastal miles, extending from the North Carolina border and Little River in the north to the ACE Basin and the Georgia border in the south, track across rivers, creeks, estuaries, sounds, bays, beaches, marshes, swamps, forests and farmland, as well as numerous cities accommodating people with a desire to live at the coast. This coast, or more specifically this coastal zone, supports fish, wildlife and ecological communities, many of which are permanently protected in parks, preserves, refuges or via private conservation easements.

While some argue that natural or maybe even supernatural forces are responsible for the great natural capital of the South Carolina coast, in truth, it was and is the people living here who forged the landscape. Early on, people treated the ecosystem that would become South Carolina as a seemingly unlimited source of fish, wildlife and land. But harvest for local consumption shifted to harvest for trade and export. Natural communities were destroyed to accommodate agriculture and settlements. Overexploitation and extinction were common drivers of further exploitation and new trade. Eventually, people—or, more importantly, the government working for people—had a strong influence in terms of environmental regulations, fish and game laws, land management and development of wildlife refuges. Throughout prehistory and history, fishing, hunting and harvest in coastal South Carolina remained a central aspect of the various cultures living on the land or near the water.

Introduction

Early in the history of South Carolina, people saw fish and wildlife populations as inherently limitless and thus could be harvested by any and all means. Of course, the idea of "limitless" was folly, but it does speak to the relatively large populations of fish and game that once existed. This book shows that overharvest always led to wildlife population declines and, beginning in the early 1700s, was followed by government regulations aimed at sustaining or augmenting fish and wildlife. This book also shows that the history of fish and game in South Carolina is complex and marked by conflict: early on, there were conflicts between Native Americans and European colonists; later, conflicts arose between the public (e.g., market hunters) and private landowners (e.g., sportsmen); and still later, conflicts arose among county, state and federal governments. However, in the end, the narrative is one of synergism where state and federal agencies and private landowners cooperate to put in place one of the most extensive and productive conservation systems currently existing on the East Coast.

Chapter 1

Defining the South Carolina Coast

SENSES OF A PLACE

A person's sense of a place is inherently biased based on what an individual views as important. A tourist standing on the beach in Myrtle Beach thinks that the coast is a narrow strip of sand suited for sunbathing and swimming. Native Americans occupying or visiting the South Carolina coast at 1000 BC viewed the coast as salt marshes and adjacent islands because here they found abundant and easily harvested fish and shellfish. European colonists in the early 1500s focused on coastal lands adjacent to rivers, bays and sounds where water depths were sufficient for ships and shipping and rivers could be used for exploration and trade. The cities of Georgetown and Charleston reflect this early bias. Following settlement, the coast was viewed as free range for hogs and cattle. And still later in the 1700s, the sense of the South Carolina coast was extended inland to include tidally influenced riverine wetlands that were eventually converted to rice cultivation.

Regardless of how people view the coast based on their own needs and preferences, the state variables of tides and water salinity universally form dynamic natural boundaries for what most consider a coastal environment. Coastal rivers in South Carolina show gradients of tidal fluctuation as far as thirty-five miles from the ocean. Likewise, salinity up coastal rivers changes from salt water to brackish to fresh water; this gradient is influenced by the volume of fresh water flowing downriver as opposed to the wedge of

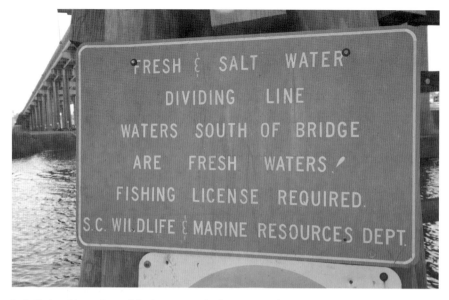

Jurisdictional boundary of fresh water and salt water on the Intracoastal Waterway near Little River. Water level and current here are controlled mainly by tidal fluctuation. *Photo by the author.*

salt water being pushed upriver by tides and winds. The South Carolina Department of Natural Resources established distinct boundaries on coastal rivers delineating fresh and salt water—these jurisdictional lines are good for regulating recreational fishing, but such boundaries are porous to coastal fish and are not generally obvious to casual observers unless marked by signs.

Recently, the need to protect environmental quality of coastal waters spawned the more comprehensive idea of a "coastal zone." The definition of the South Carolina Coastal Zone was stimulated by passage of the federal Coastal Zone Management Act in 1972 and was developed under the South Carolina Coastal Tidelands and Wetlands Act beginning in 1977 (1977, 48-39-10). The broad purpose of this legislation was effective protection and management of coastal resources. In South Carolina, protection of the coast focuses on defined "Critical Areas": coastal waters, tidelands, beaches and dunes. And thus, the South Carolina Coastal Zone includes "all coastal waters and submerged lands seaward to the State's jurisdictional limits and all lands and waters in the counties of the State which contain any one or more of the critical areas. The counties are Beaufort, Berkeley, Charleston, Colleton, Dorchester, Horry, Jasper and Georgetown." The seaward jurisdictional limit of the South Carolina Coastal Zone extends three miles. The South Carolina Department of Health and Environmental Control (SCDHEC) is responsible for implementing the state's Coastal Management Program and manages environmental quality. In contrast, the South Carolina Department of Natural Resources is responsible for implementing and enforcing fish and game regulations in the South Carolina Coastal Zone and statewide.

The current geopolitical definition of the South Carolina Coastal Zone is not without problems. Specifically, some rivers flowing to the coast have their origins outside coastal counties and thus may fall under relaxed regulation allowing pollutants to reach coastal waters.[1]

The solution here is to include entire watersheds in the South Carolina Coastal Zone, but this will likely be a difficult political path. Another problem is the establishment of tidal riverine wetland boundaries, as the historical building of dikes for rice cultivation and the subsequent decay of these dikes called into question whether the lands were privately or publicly owned. This complex environmental and property issue reviewed by Wyche will be considered later in this book.

Future changes to the boundaries of the South Carolina Coastal Zone are likely as global warming leads to a rising sea level. Recent models predict that South Carolina will see a 1.2-foot increase in sea level by 2050 and a 4.0-foot increase by 2100.[2] The broad effect will extend the South

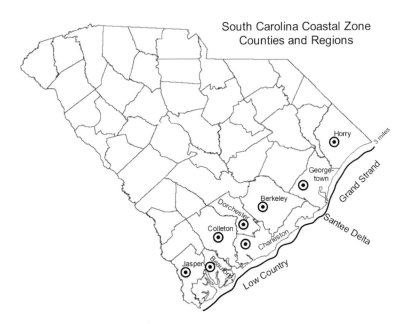

CHART 1. Counties of the South Carolina Coastal Zone and the three-mile seaward limit. *Image background from d-maps.com.*

Rising sea level and erosion of coastal land may affect the nature and extent of the South Carolina Coastal Zone in the future. *Courtesy U.S. Fish and Wildlife Service.*

Carolina Coastal Zone landward with shorter return periods and increased magnitudes of flooding events. Such changes have indeed occurred in the past, but the current spate of sea level rise is unprecedented due to global warming caused by destruction of forests and burning of fossil fuels.

Three segments of the South Carolina Coastal Zone are identified based on geophysical and cultural properties:

1. NORTHERN OR GRAND STRAND. This segment extends roughly sixty miles from the border of North Carolina to Winyah Bay and Georgetown. It is a crescent-shaped area of shallow ocean waters and broad beaches. There are few inlets, and salt marshes behind the barrier islands are relatively narrow. Here the Waccamaw River, an unregulated tidal blackwater river, skirts the coast and flows southwest, eventually joining the Great Pee Dee and Black Rivers at Winyah Bay. The Northern segment includes Myrtle Beach and the Grand Strand, popular destinations for tourists and retirees.

2. MIDDLE OR SANTEE DELTA. This segment of roughly twenty miles extends from Winyah Bay to Bulls Bay and McClellanville. It includes the broad delta formed from sediments deposited by the Santee River. The physical structure of this area was highly modified as a result of an upriver dam forming Lake Marion.

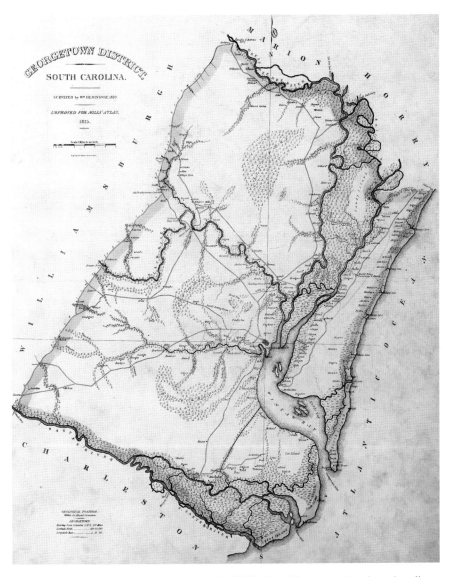

Map of the Georgetown District from the 1825 *Mills' Atlas*. Numerous rice plantations line the lower reaches of the Waccamaw River. *Courtesy Library of Congress.*

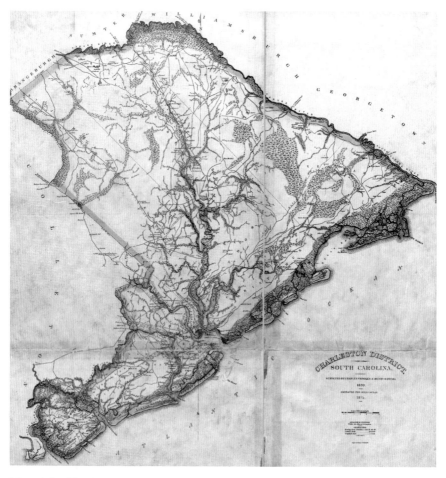

Map of the Charleston District from the 1825 *Mills' Atlas*. Charleston Harbor is the center of commerce. *Courtesy Library of Congress.*

3. SOUTHERN OR LOWCOUNTRY. This segment of about 110 miles extends from Bulls Bay to the Savannah River. It includes Charleston and numerous small islands in a complex matrix of extensive marshes and tidal creeks. Major rivers reaching the ocean in this segment include the Wando, Cooper, Ashley, Stono and Edisto Rivers near Charleston and the Bull, Coosaw and Broad Rivers near Beaufort.

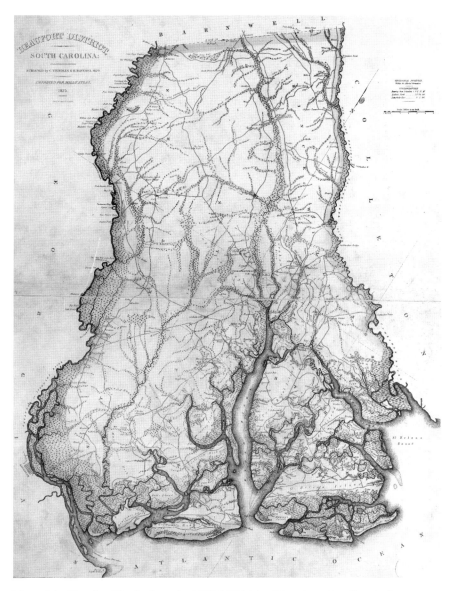

Map of the Beaufort District from the 1825 *Mills' Atlas*. Rice plantations line the lower reaches of the Broad River. *Courtesy Library of Congress.*

OWNERSHIP OF A PLACE

In a place like the South Carolina Coastal Zone, where land and water intertwine, the issue of ownership can be complicated but is central to an understanding of historical and modern fish and game regulation. In the simplest case, the State of South Carolina has jurisdiction over territorial waters extending from the low water line of the coast in direct contact with the open sea to three miles seaward. Application of this rule is relatively straightforward on the northern coast, where long, linear beaches meet the ocean, but requires some modification on the southern coast, where numerous inlets, rivers and islands create a punctuated baseline. Establishing ownership of internal waters, those located landward from territorial waters, is still more complicated due to extensive creeks, mudflats and wetlands subject to tidal ebb and flow. Controversies over ownership of such areas in coastal South Carolina have historically involved the right to harvest fish and shellfish, the right to manage or hunt waterfowl, the right to obstruct navigation and the right to dredge or fill. These rights, when exercised, have potentially far-reaching negative impacts on marine and freshwater ecosystems due to the importance of tidelands to populations of coastal fish and wildlife.

Internal or inland waters of South Carolina fell under English common law in 1663, when Charles II granted the new province of Carolina to eight of his trusted friends, the lord proprietors. The charter of Carolina was quite specific in terms of both coastal geographic features and fishing rights. This reflected the importance of fish and commercial fishing in English culture and the efforts by the proprietors to claim any and all natural resources of potential economic value.

> [T]ogether with all and singular ports, harbours, bays, rivers, isles and islets belonging to the country aforesaid…lakes, rivers, bays and islets, scituate or being within the bounds or limits aforesaid, with the fishing of all sorts of fish, whales, sturgeons and all other royal fishes in the sea, bays, islets and rivers within the premises, and the fish therein taken.[3]

The lord proprietors from 1663 to 1719, the royal governors from 1719 to 1776 and South Carolina beginning in 1776 all made grants of land and water to private individuals and companies in efforts to encourage settlement, to stimulate commerce and to drive out the Native Americans. This land grant process effectively ended with the Civil War. In South

Murrells Inlet tidal creek at low tide. *Photo by the author.*

The same Murrells Inlet tidal creek at high tide. *Photo by the author.*

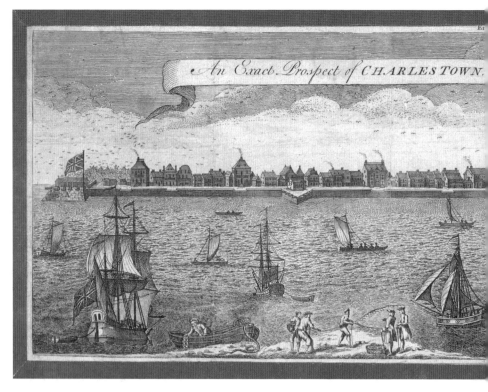

A 1762 depiction of Charlestown harbor. Men are netting fish and collecting oysters in the foreground. Flocks of unidentified birds fly from the forests surrounding the town. *Courtesy Library of Congress.*

Carolina, some land grants clearly caused problems for the public interest in navigation and fisheries, as indicated by a 1726 act establishing fines for obstructing creeks with downed timber (1726, 519). The same act also established fines for poisoning creeks in order to catch fish. Several aspects of this 1726 act are noteworthy. First, it was written soon after the end of the proprietary government and marked the first attempt at natural resource management by a government in the province of South Carolina. (The proprietary government largely failed to regulate issues related to natural resources.) Second, it stipulated different modes of punishment for white persons and enslaved people, a common practice in most early fish and game regulations.

Over time, land grants of waters and tidelands were curtailed and ownership of internal waters by the prevailing government or state was established as a public trust for the public good.[4] Specifically, the state

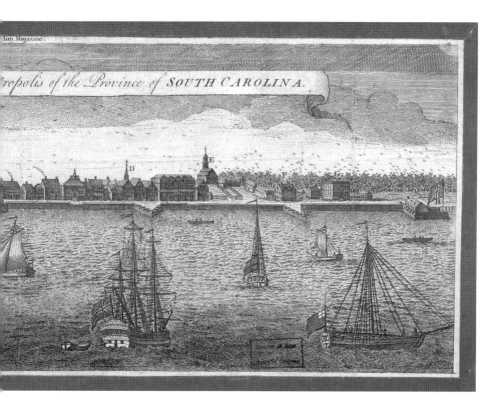

claims all submerged lands, areas below the low-water mark in navigable waters. The state also claims all navigable waters. Furthermore, the state claims tidelands, the area between the high-water mark and low-water mark, adjacent navigable waters. The establishment of this ownership landscape sets the stage for writing acts and laws limiting fishing methods, seasons and take.

Numerous recent court battles were waged over property rights on land/water existing below the high-water mark.[5] In some cases, property rights were upheld, but only when the original land grant was specific in terms of aquatic boundaries or other features. In the absence of such proof, property rights were not upheld, and land use reverted *prima facie* to the public trust. Furthermore, the use of the term *navigable* in defining waters of the state led to legal challenges, as the amount of water needed to float a boat varies greatly depending on the boat. Recent court actions in South Carolina defined navigable waters in terms of connection and the ability to support valuable floatage (1976, 49-1-10). The importance of hunting and fishing in the South Carolina culture was affirmed when such actions were included in the definition of valuable floatage.

In colonial South Carolina, lands existing above the high-water mark were populated by Europeans via the land grant process, but this process did not generally recognize Native American landownership. However, there was some recognition by the colonial government of Native American rights to hunt and fish. In contrast to England, where firearms and hunting were generally limited to the noble class, hunting rights were fully extended to the colonists and to enslaved people. The narrative of interaction between Native Americans and Europeans regarding property rights initially involved peaceful cooperation and trade. In the early and mid-1700s, Native Americans supplied a lucrative market for deerskins, many of which were delivered to what was then named Charlestown and shipped to England. However, as the European population increased and natural resources dwindled due to overlap of what Greer has termed the indigenous commons and colonial commons, commerce shifted to agriculture and livestock. The plight of Native Americans became dire. Their populations were decimated by disease and forced emigration. Their hunting and agricultural lands were lost via acquiescence, payment, negotiation and aggression. A recent study by Coughlan and Nelson showed that abandoned Native American settlements and fields were among the first areas claimed by Europeans via the land grant process.

Although landownership and land grants entailed official establishment of property boundaries and recording of deeds, rural land in coastal South Carolina prior to the early and mid-1700s was essentially free range, representing a unique type of colonial commons used for hunting and raising livestock. But beginning in the late 1700s, the free range started to become less free, as the land use of hunting came into conflict with the land use of raising livestock. Specifically, the practice of setting the woods on fire at night to drive deer toward hunters was banned in 1769 due to high accidental livestock mortality (1769, 988). At about this time, the first legislation emerges addressing the issue of trespass on private land for hunting. Subsequent laws and ordinances over the next one hundred years requiring fencing and enclosure of livestock, as well as restricting access of hunters to private lands, meant that by the end of Civil War, the colonial commons had been largely replaced by a privately owned and fenced patchwork landscape highly modified by timbering and agriculture. Exceptions to this were dense swamps of coastal South Carolina that initially resisted modification.

Because the state claimed ownership of navigable waters for the public interest, regulation of fishing started earlier in South Carolina and was more widespread than regulation of hunting. But soon after the Civil War, when unregulated market hunting and harvest in coastal South Carolina led to widespread declines in wildlife populations, there were numerous attempts to limit such activities on private land. Most of these efforts were moot as no enforcement personnel were in place. Fish wardens with the job of enforcing regulations did not appear until 1878 (1878, 600). Game wardens entered the scene much later in 1905 (1905, 489). But even with wardens and more regulations in place, fish and wildlife populations continued to spiral downward because there were no wildlife refuges.

Wildlife refuges represent the ultimate approach for managing fish and wildlife in the public interest. Such refuges convey to the state certain property rights in efforts to protect wildlife populations from harvest but also, more importantly, to protect the reproductive activities of these wildlife populations during critical times and in critical places. The first game sanctuaries in South Carolina were envisioned in 1926 with an act that authorized the chief game warden to enter into agreements with private landowners so "game, birds, and animals may breed, unmolested." This was no-cost legislation, but it marked an important turning point in coastal conservation efforts. At about the same time, the federal government also

ACE Basin National Estuarine Research Reserve. *Courtesy National Oceanic and Atmospheric Administration.*

began acquiring lands to be placed in national wildlife refuges, but the federal approach was one of land acquisition: a complete transfer of land from the private domain to the public domain in efforts to protect the public trust. It was not until 1941 that the State of South Carolina begin acquiring land for conservation in an approach similar to that used by the federal government (i.e., purchasing land from private or corporate landowners).

From 1926 to the 1970s, coastal South Carolina, because it was relatively undeveloped and still supported vast areas of natural communities important for migrating fish and wildlife, was the focus of numerous efforts to acquire land for conservation or to place land under specific restrictions. Table 1 below shows the current distribution of state heritage preserves, state wildlife management areas, bird sanctuaries and federal wildlife refuges. The list is lengthy but would be longer if it included protected lands in state and county parks or those placed under conservation easements (i.e., places where private landowners have given up certain property rights in the interest of conservation). Currently, about 30 percent of coastal South Carolina is under some type of conservation protection.[6] While some have postulated that the high quality of fish and wildlife habitat now in coastal South Carolina refuges was the direct result of sound wildlife management by prior landowners, particularly those managing hunting preserves, the historical record reveals a more complex narrative.

Table 1. National Wildlife Refuges, Wildlife Management Areas and Heritage Preserves located in coastal South Carolina (sites arranged geographically)

County	Property Name	Acreage	Ownership	Hunting	Fishing
Horry	Cartwheel Bay Heritage Preserve/WMA	568	state	yes	no
Horry	Lewis Ocean Bay Heritage Preserve/WMA	10,427	state	yes	no
Horry and Georgetown	Waccamaw National Wildlife Refuge	29,000	federal	yes	yes
Horry	Waccamaw River Heritage Preserve/WMA	5,347	state	yes	yes

County	Property Name	Acreage	Ownership	Hunting	Fishing
Georgetown	North Santee Bar Seabird Sanctuary	variable	state	no	no
Georgetown	Samworth Wildlife Management Area	1,588	state	yes	yes
Georgetown	Santee Delta Wildlife Management Area	1,722	state	yes	yes
Georgetown	Tom Yawkey Wildlife Center/ WMA	24,000	state	no	no
Charleston	Bird Key— Stono Seabird Sanctuary	variable	state	no	no
Charleston	Botany Bay Plantation Heritage Preserve/WMA	3,363	state	yes	yes
Charleston	Buzzard Island Heritage Preserve	variable	state	no	no
Charleston	Cape Romain National Wildlife Refuge	66,287	federal	yes	yes
Charleston	Capers Island Heritage Preserve	2,254	state	no	yes
Charleston	Crab Bank Seabird Sanctuary	variable	state	no	no
Charleston	Deveaux Bank Seabird Sanctuary	variable	state	no	no
Charleston	Dugannon Plantation Heritage Preserve/WMA	643	state	yes	no

COUNTY	PROPERTY NAME	ACREAGE	OWNERSHIP	HUNTING	FISHING
Charleston	Fort Lamar Heritage Preserve	14	state	no	no
Charleston	Lighthouse Inlet Heritage Preserve	100	state	no	no
Charleston	Santee Coastal Reserve Wildlife Management Area	24,000	state	yes	yes
Berkeley	Bonneau Ferry Wildlife Management Area	10,712	state	yes	yes
Berkeley	Canal Wildlife Management Area	2,491	federal/ state	yes	yes
Berkeley	Childsbury Towne Heritage Preserve	90	state	no	yes
Berkeley	Francis Marion National Forest	258,816	federal	yes	yes
Berkeley	Hatchery Wildlife Management Area	2,400	state	yes	yes
Berkeley	Moultrie Hunt Unit Wildlife Management Area	9,480	state	yes	yes
Dorchester	Edisto River Wildlife Management Area	1,375	state	yes	no
Colleton	Bear Island Wildlife Management Area	12,021	state	yes	yes
Colleton	Crosby Oxypolis Heritage Preserve	32	state	no	no

County	Property Name	Acreage	Ownership	Hunting	Fishing
Colleton	Donnelley Wildlife Management Area	8,048	state	yes	no
Colleton	South Fenwick Island	400	state	no	no
Colleton	St. Helena Sound Heritage Preserve/WMA	10,301	state	yes	yes
Beaufort	Altamaha Towne Heritage Preserve	100	state	no	no
Beaufort	Bay Point Shoal Seabird Sanctuary	variable	state	no	no
Beaufort	Daws Island Heritage Preserve	1,881	state	no	yes
Beaufort, Charleston, Colleton	Ernest F. Hollings ACE Basin National Wildlife Refuge	12,000	federal	yes	yes
Beaufort	Fort Frederick Heritage Preserve	3	state	no	no
Beaufort	Greens Shell Enclosure Heritage Preserve	3	city/state	no	no
Beaufort	Joiner Bank Seabird Sanctuary	variable	state	no	no
Beaufort	Old Island Heritage Preserve/WMA	400	state	yes	yes
Beaufort	Pinckney Island National Wildlife Refuge	4,053	federal	yes	yes
Beaufort	South Bluff Heritage Preserve	24	state	no	no
Beaufort	Stoney Creek Battery Heritage Preserve	1	state	no	no

COUNTY	PROPERTY NAME	ACREAGE	OWNERSHIP	HUNTING	FISHING
Beaufort	Victoria Bluff Heritage Preserve	977	state	yes	no
Jasper	Savannah National Wildlife Refuge	31,551	federal	yes	yes
Jasper	Tillman Sand Ridge Heritage Preserve	1,422	state	yes	no
Jasper	Turtle Island Wildlife Management Area	1,700	state	yes	no
Jasper	Tybee Island National Wildlife Refuge	400	federal	no	no

Chapter 2

Native American Fishing and Hunting

BEFORE THE EUROPEANS

It is, of course, difficult to assess methods and impacts of Native American fishing and hunting in coastal South Carolina prior to European contact due to the absence of written accounts. Instead, anthropologists rely on artifacts giving some sense of how these people interacted with their environments; such evidence is available only in a few places. We know that the Native Americans first encountered by Europeans on the South Carolina coast were the product of an exodus from Asia. They crossed the Bering land bridge in Alaska about 18,000 BC, made possible by falling sea levels, and then fanned out as nomads across North America, supported by hunting of the Pleistocene megafauna (e.g., mammoths, mastodons, sloths, saber-toothed cats and others). As the climate warmed toward the end of the Pleistocene, many large animals went extinct (about 11,000 BC), and it is currently a topic of great debate whether Paleoindians drove these animals to extinction by overhunting or whether animal populations declined due to a rapidly changing climate; according to Broughton and Weitzel, it was likely a combination of both factors.

During the Pleistocene, ecological communities of coastal South Carolina included a mix of wetlands, savannah and forest similar to the present. However, the positions of these likely shifted, as sea levels were lower during this time. Animal communities, as indicated by collection of fossils on Edisto

Island, included many of the same species as today, with the addition of the walrus, capybara, ground sloth, tapir, dire wolf, peccary, mastodon, mammoth and other large mammals.[7] It is impossible to determine from available evidence if these animals were hunted on the coast by Native Americans, although a few spear and arrow points from this period have been found in coastal South Carolina.

During the Archaic period (8000–1000 BC), Native Americans shifted their diets more toward fish, small game and plants. They began using a variety of tools made from stone, bone and shell and also crafted pottery for cooking and food storage. It is during this period that we see first clear evidence of a Native American culture in coastal South Carolina based on harvest of fish and shellfish from marshes. (Earlier, Native American occupation in South Carolina was concentrated in uplands or in river valleys of inland areas; these tribes visited the coast only sporadically.) The tribes that harvested shellfish and then built raised circular structures made of shell (i.e., shell rings) may be some of the earliest in coastal South Carolina to construct permanent dwellings in close association with a natural food source.

Shell rings are found in seventeen locations along the coast of South Carolina. They are always located adjacent to or in salt marshes and may be ring- or C-shaped. In all cases, coastal erosion through time has modified the original structures, but at present, average maximum diameter is about sixty meters with heights ranging from one to three meters.[8] Shell rings are constructed mostly from oysters but may also include clams, fish bones, pottery, tools and even human remains. The shell rings in South Carolina were constructed about 2000 BC and have various explanations.

Early interpretations viewed shell rings simply as refuse dumps of Native Americans or as fish traps. However, recent excavations suggest that shell rings and middens may represent complex shellworks that elevated the living surface above the marsh surface and thus allowed Native Americans to establish long-term residences characterized by social organization. These same areas were also associated with feasts and large ceremonies. The size and extent of some shell rings suggest that building materials were not just from shellfish harvest but were instead excavated from other sites and transported in a planned effort to build monuments.[9]

The Woodland period (about 1000 BC–AD 1100) was marked by more extensive use of ceramics and a broadening of the diet to frequently include white-tailed deer, bear and reptiles, as well as fish and shellfish. Quasi-permanent settlements were extensive, while small bands of hunter/

Oysters in tidal creeks represent one of the first coastal species to be heavily harvested and were readily accessible to Native Americans. *Photo by the author.*

Pieces of pottery intermixed with oyster shells comprising the Sewee Shell Ring. *Photo by the author.*

Sewee Shell Ring at the edge of a salt marsh located in the Francis Marion National Forest. Through time, red cedar trees colonized the shell substrate. *Photo by the author.*

gatherers ranged seasonally to augment food resources. It is during this period that burial and ceremony mounds emerged.

The Mississippian period (about AD 1100–1550) saw increasingly complex social organization and the emergence of chiefdoms among Native Americans living at or near the coast. Large permanent villages emerged, and agriculture focused on growing corn, beans and squash. Agricultural fields were typically in river valleys and adjacent to villages. Native American farming involved separation of labor and certain aspects of landownership. Despite the growing of crops, fishing, hunting and seasonal foraging continued.

At the time of widespread European contact, populations of Native Americans numbered in the millions throughout what would become the United States. On the South Carolina coast, there were numerous tribes that could be roughly divided into two loose groups or associations: a confederacy of Siouan-derived tribes north of Charles Town that lived along rivers and a confederacy of tribes, the Cusabo, that lived on the south coast and were derived from Creeks. An unrelated collection of tribes also lived along the Savannah River.[10] With such high populations and concentration of people in temporary or permanent settlements, it is useful to examine impacts on the natural environment prior to European

Clam mound located in the general vicinity of the Sewee Shell Ring. *Photo by the author.*

contact. There is a general mythology that Native American actions on the land were benign and thus when the first European explorers landed at the coast, they found a pristine, undisturbed environment. However, Cronon and White debunked this myth. Tree clearing with axes or fire, initially concentrated in river floodplains but later extended to uplands, created extensive fields and grasslands in various stages of forest succession. Trees were removed not just to prepare the land for agriculture but also to supply building materials for shelters, houses and canoes. This extensive environmental change greatly increased erosion and sent large loads of sediments flowing into rivers and streams.[11]

Perhaps most importantly, Native Americans modified the environment and managed game with fire. The specific goals for setting fire varied both temporally and geographically. Paleoindians used fire primarily to aid in hunting. They used circles or lines of fire to drive game toward geographic features, where it could be concentrated and then dispatched. During the Archaic period, fire continued to be used for driving game but was also directed at creating openings and forest structure conducive to certain game species such as white-tailed deer. With the expenditure of effort in managing game, hunting lands assumed a type of ownership by tribes but were also often

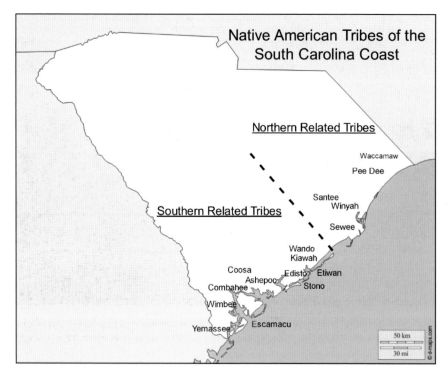

CHART 2. Native American tribes originally occupying the South Carolina coast. *Redrawn from sciway.net and Waddell; image background from d-maps.com.*

the source of conflict between tribes. In the Woodland and Mississippian periods, fire was used to clear land for agriculture.[12] The frequent use of fire by Native Americans in the Southeast created a landscape that was relatively open and dominated by fire-dependent plant species. As such, longleaf pine savannas dominated most of the American south when Europeans first landed. Prescribed burning is now a standard management technique used to restore longleaf pine ecosystems and to manage game species in coastal South Carolina.

Prior to European contact, Native American hunting of larger animals was via bow and arrow or spear. The spear was made more effective with the development of a spear thrower, or atlatl. In addition, Irwin maintains that small game was killed with blow guns typically used by children or via snares, pitfall traps, deadfall traps, or by clubbing. Much of what we know about hunting methods is based on Native Americans residing in eastern inland forests, as populations here were higher and thus the availability of artifacts is also higher. We know very little about pre-European hunting methods

Pine forest in coastal South Carolina soon after a recent prescribed fire. Native Americans set fires to encourage certain game species and to facilitate travel and agriculture. *Photo by the author.*

Open understory of grasses emerging in a coastal South Carolina pine forest one year after fire. *Photo by the author.*

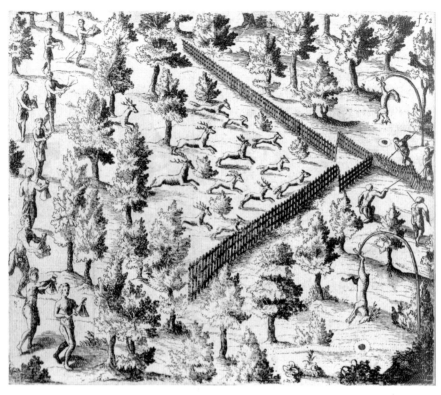

Above: A 1613 depiction of northeast Native Americans driving deer toward a fenced enclosure. Driving deer with noise or fire was a common hunting practice. *Courtesy Library of Congress.*

Left: Florida Native Americans in the 1500s disguised under deerskin. This hunting method was used for approaching deer within bow and arrow range. *Courtesy Library of Congress.*

Archaic period projectile points (*left*) and woodland period projectile points (*right*) from coastal South Carolina. *Courtesy Horry County Museum.*

of Native Americans who lived at the South Carolina coast, although we can assume that their approaches were like Native Americans living inland. Native Americans hunted big game by ambushing, calling, decoying, driving and stalking. Fire was used to drive or corral deer,[13] but there is also evidence that Native Americans hunted deer from trees.[14]

Projectile points, because they are well preserved and widely collected, offer the best available evidence for understanding different Native American hunting cultures. These points, typically made of flint or chert, were shaped by the process of knapping and reflect continuous improvements in penetration potential, durability and attachment to the shafts of arrows or spears. Projectile points were important objects of trade among Native American tribes, as the necessary stone was limited in availability.

Methods of Native American fishing prior to European contact are more difficult to determine due to the absence of artifacts or long-lasting legacies, but it is generally presumed by Waddell that coastal populations made greater use of fish and shellfish than those living inland because soils at the coast were sandy and less productive of crops.[15] The presence of shell middens up and down the coast suggests either permanent or occasional but intense use of shellfish. Native Americans also made good use of nets, bone hooks, traps and spears. There is anecdotal evidence that Native Americans used parts of black walnut, yellow buckeye and goat's rue to stun or poison fish when confined to small pools in streams. Weirs were also constructed from stones to corral fish, but remnants of these are found only in mountain

A 1585 depiction of Native American fishing on the coast of North Carolina. The painting, by John White, shows spears, nets and traps deployed for sharks, sturgeon and various invertebrates. *Courtesy National Archives.*

streams. The exception is a large fish weir under present-day Boston that was constructed by Native Americans from wood stakes during the Archaic period. Decima and Dincauze concluded it was designed to corral and capture marine fish in a shallow tidal creek setting.

EUROPEAN CONTACT AND EARLY COLONIZATION

The first ship landing in the vicinity of coastal South Carolina came from Hispaniola in 1520. Lucas Vázquez de Ayllón was associated with this voyage, and when the boat sailed into a favorable harbor, the Spaniards were met by a group of Native Americans. The explorers took some hostages, as one of the reasons for exploration was procurement of slaves for sugar cane plantations in the Caribbean. This began a lengthy process of Native American exploitation by the Europeans. The 1520 landing, another in 1525 by Vázquez and a subsequent one by the French explorer Jean Ribault in 1562 at Port Royal all attempted permanent settlement at the South Carolina coast, but the efforts were not successful. It was not until 1567 that Spain was able to establish a base at Sante Elena, which flourished for about twenty years; it also was eventually abandoned due to persistent conflicts with Native Americans, the French and the English. Widespread European settlement waned and did not resume until about one hundred years later.

There are glimpses of ecological conditions and wildlife along the South Carolina coast via narratives written by early European explorers. These descriptions were influenced by almost universal Native American interactions and suggest ubiquitous occupation of the coast at the time of European colonization. Ribault in 1562 went ashore near Port Royal and described large populations of turkeys, quail and deer; his crew easily netted fish. On that same excursion, they encountered Native Americans roasting a bobcat but also later described a culture based on corn, acorns, turkeys and deer.[16] This is consistent with Mississippian Native American culture throughout the state. In 1664, William Hilton and his party landed near Port Royal and observed a great abundance of food available to the Native Americans: corn, pumpkins, squash, grapes, figs, deer, turkeys, quail, waterfowl, fish and shellfish. The Native Americans provided the explorers with mullet, bass and shad; on one day, the explorers themselves killed four swans, ten geese, twenty cranes, ten turkeys, forty ducks, thirty-five parakeets and various other wading birds.[17] Many of the early explorers of the Carolina coast in the mid-1600s described relatively open forests of large trees presumably maintained by fire, fields of corn, Native American settlements and an abundance of fish and wildlife, suggesting that human populations were relatively small and that overharvest was not yet a facet of coastal life.[18]

By the late 1600s, however, the role of the Native American hunter in coastal South Carolina had already begun to shift. In 1682, Samuel Wilson wrote about the province of Carolina:

> *The woods abound with Hares, Squirrels, Raccoons, Possums, Conyes and Deer, which last are so plenty that an Indian hunter hath kill'd nine fatt Deere in a day all shott by himself, and all the considerable Planters have an Indian hunter which they hire for less than twenty shillings a year, and one hunter will very well find a Family of thirty people with as much Venison and Foul, as they can eat.*[19]

Following European contact, Native Americans quickly adopted guns, and their hunting skills were valued in terms of currency. Guns and other items such as blankets, cloth, liquor and metal utensils were often traded for deerskins, setting in motion rapid change of the Native American culture on the coast. The proprietary government viewed this arrangement as one that could generate great profit but Murphy concluded it was limited by conflicts and logistics.

THE DEERSKIN TRADE

Among coastal Native Americans, deerskins were a ubiquitous commodity used for a wide range of objects: laces, belts, pouches, moccasins, clothing and drumheads. Deerskins initially were presented to European explorers as a sign of friendship, but this commodity quickly assumed new value, particularly as consumers in Europe began viewing buckskin as fashionable and extremely useful. 1674 was considered the beginning of substantial deerskin trading when Dr. Henry Woodward signed a treaty with the Westo Native Americans living near the Savannah River.[20] Because the deerskin trade was so lucrative, not surprisingly, conflicts soon arose among Native Americans, traders and the proprietary government. Deerskin trading quickly spread to other tribes at the coast, then to other tribes in South

Carolina and then as far east as the Mississippi River. Charles Town was initially the home base for deerskin traders and the major port where deerskins were shipped to England, but Braund suggested that exports from Savannah, Georgia, eventually rivaled those of Charles Town.

The deerskin trade was a major economic driver of an emergent South Carolina economy, but Stern maintained that many aspects of the enterprise were negative. Initially, deerskin trading was intertwined with Native American slave trading, a practice that was eventually banned but still created much animosity among Native American tribes. Deerskin traders were often unscrupulous in trading and finance. These and other grievances spawned the Yamasee War in 1715, a violent conflict that significantly set back colonial progress in agriculture and livestock raising. Perhaps most importantly, the deerskin enterprise revealed the inability of the proprietary government to govern, as many regulations focused on the deerskin enterprise were simply ignored.

The deerskin trade in the Southeast and other parts of the country represents one of the first examples of market harvest leading to extirpation of an animal population. Braund compiled various data and estimated that from 1698 to 1715, about 53,000 deerskins were annually exported from Charles Town. By 1759, this export statistic was up to 236,000. As a comparison, the total South Carolina deer harvest in 2018 was 194,000. Surprisingly, the decline of deer populations in the United States was relatively slow up until the time of the Revolutionary War. This can perhaps be explained by the fact that forest clearing for agriculture created more edge habitats conducive to deer. However, even with this benefit, after the Revolutionary War, deer population decline accelerated, probably due to unregulated hunting and habitat destruction; by the early 1900s, deer were nearly gone. Their population recovery was the result of game laws and intense restoration efforts by state and federal wildlife biologists.

The deerskin trade is often described in terms of how it shifted the behavior of Native American men from subsistence hunting to market hunting. This in turn also shifted the traditional food production systems, as the men were increasing absent from settlements. Paveo-Zuckerman hypothesized that the deerskin trade hindered the raising of domesticated livestock by the Creeks, thus making them vulnerable to extirpation. Braund expanded this analysis, tracing the almost complete reorganization of Creek culture, thus making them dependent on English goods. When prices for deerskins eventually dropped and deer populations dwindled, Native Americans shifted their actions toward selling other items to the British.

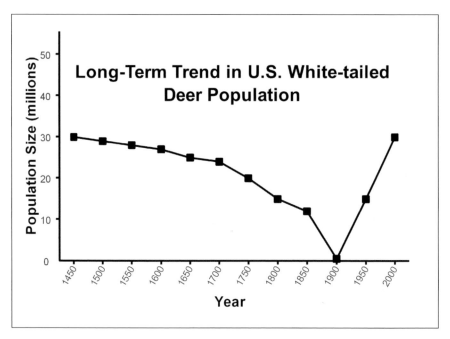

CHART 3. Long-term trend in the U.S. white-tailed deer population. White-tailed deer were nearly extinct by 1900 due to unregulated hunting and habitat destruction. *Redrawn from data compiled by deerfriendly.com.*

THE KNOWLEDGE TRADE

Many of the early colonists arriving in South Carolina were planters from the West Indies. They brought with them numerous African slaves and were knowledgeable regarding agriculture and survival in the Caribbean. However, coastal South Carolina posed new challenges in terms of navigation and food procurement. Initially, Native Americans at the coast were employed as guides by the planters; later, they were employed as hunters and fishermen. Their knowledge regarding local wildlife populations and how to harvest this wildlife in South Carolina was acquired by trade, purchase or observation.

Native American use of the dugout canoe was common at the coast. It was a boat that allowed them to navigate the shallow coastal creeks and rivers for purposes of fishing and trade. Harris maintained that the basic building block of a dugout canoe was expanded to a raft by lashing thus increasing stability and cargo load. Although it is assumed that coastal Native Americans made extensive use of fish and shellfish via gathering

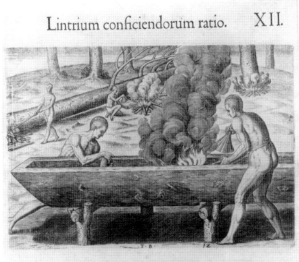

Lintrium conficiendorum ratio.   XII.

Ira est in VIRGINIA cymbas fabricandi ratio: nam, cum ferreis instrumentis aut aliis nostris similibus careant, eas tamen pa arc ni-runt nostris non minus commodas ad nauigandum quo lubet per flumi-na & ad piscandum. Primum arbore aliqua crassa & alta delecta, pro cymba quam parare volunt magnitudine, ignem circa eius radices summa tellure in ambitu struunt ex arborum musco bene resiccato, & ligni assulis paulatim ignem excitantes, ne flamma altius ascendat, & arboris longitudinem minuat. Pene adusta & ruinam minante arbo-re, nouum suscitant ignem, quem flagrare sinunt, donec arbor sponte cadat. Adustis deinde arbo-ris fastigio & ramis, vt truncus iustam longitudinem retineat, tignis transuersis supra furcas po-sitis imponunt, ea altitudine vt commode laborare possint, tunc cortice conchis quibusdam adem-pto, integriorem trunci partem pro cymba inferiore parte seruant, in altera parte ignem secundum trunci longitudinem struunt, praeterquam extremis, quod satis adustum illis videtur, restincto igne conchis scabunt, & nouo suscitato igne denuo adurunt, atque ita deinceps pergunt, subinde vren-tes & scabentes, donec cymba necessarium alueum nacta sit. Sic Domini spiritus rudibus homini-bus sug gerit rationem, qua res in suum vsum necessarias conficere queant.

B 4

A 1590 depiction of Native Americans making a dugout canoe by burning and scraping with seashells. *Courtesy National Archives.*

from the shore and from canoe, the archaeological remains of this are sparse, likely because of the organic nature of their equipment. But clearly, explorers learned fishing approaches from the Native Americans, as indicated by the narrative of Maurice Mathews during a 1680 expedition to the Ashley River area.

> *In all parts of the rivers and creeks wee never want fish of severall sorts which wee and our Indians doe catch with netts, hooks, weirs, and by shooting them with arrowes. The fish wee have are Sturgeon, Bass, drum, Mullet, plaice, Trouts, Jacks, Cattfish.*[21]

Likewise, African American slaves in coastal South Carolina quickly meshed fishing methods used in West Africa (e.g., nets, baskets, poisoning and weirs) with methods used by Native Americans to harvest local fish for consumption and sale. A group of enslaved people known as "fishing negroes" dominated fishing in and around Charleston. They plied the local waters in dugout canoes, and a special fish market was eventually constructed for their direct sales.[22] Commercial fishing around Charleston continued to expand and was dominated by African American fishermen at least until 1880.[23] It is interesting to note that fish poisoning, a method commonly practiced by Native Americans living inland, was apparently so common in South Carolina that a 1726 law (1726, 519) banned the practice. African Americans apparently brought the practice of fish poisoning from the West Indies, where they used mixtures of quicklime and plant extracts to stun fish in small pools.[24]

Settlers in coastal South Carolina also borrowed from Native Americans the use of fire to manage vegetation for agriculture and apparently also for hunting. The practices of fire hunting and driving of deer at night with torches became common in the early 1700s. When these fires turned intense, apparently many cattle and other livestock were accidentally killed. When deer were concentrated by these fires and shooting ensued at night, the hunters themselves also suffered much mortality. In response, the royal government passed an act in 1769 banning deer hunting at night with torches (1769, 988); a similar act was passed in 1789 that again addressed hunting at night with fire (1789, 1463).

Chapter 3

Settlement and the Environment

EARLY FISH AND GAME REGULATION

European colonists coming to South Carolina were encouraged by land grants and other financial incentives. Their motives in the New World were focused on extracting and exploiting natural resources. Many colonists came with a basket full of rights not granted in their home countries: fishing, hunting, landownership and timber cutting. Further, they could freely exercise these rights in a nearly nonexistent regulatory landscape. As such, environmental change was rapid and extensive.

The first wave of environmental change in coastal South Carolina was associated with the introduction of hogs and cattle. Under the proprietary government, livestock represented a way to turn a quick profit, as the animals could be released into the woods or marshes, where they foraged in what was initially free range. Enslaved people figured prominently in the herding and tending of South Carolina livestock, as many of them came with prior experience from the coast of Africa.[25] Because Native Americans frequently burned the forests, the understory was a grass-dominated savannah (sometimes called "Horse Savannah") conducive to movement and rapid growth of cattle.[26] South Carolina quickly became a center of the livestock industry in the late 1600s, and herds of cattle were driven from the coast westward.[27] Pork and beef became important exports to the West Indies, New England and Europe.[28]

Free-ranging cattle, like these near Georgetown in the early 1900s, were brought to coastal South Carolina by European colonists and were fattened on the grasses that dominated pine forests influenced by frequent fire. *Courtesy Georgetown County Library.*

A second wave of environmental change was associated with the planters who either occupied agricultural land previously cleared by Native Americans or who began clearing forests themselves. The longleaf pine that dominated the coastal savannahs was cut for lumber. The bark of living trees was removed and the oozing resin collected. This spawned a naval stores industry of pitch and tar but eventually led to the death of the trees. Hardwood forests were cut for firewood or the sale of various wood products. Much of the hard work of clearing New World forests was done by enslaved people, but big profits were elusive due a persistent labor shortage.[29]

Kawashima and Tone suggest that efforts to regulate tree cutting in the colonies were more common in the North than in South Carolina. However, one of the first efforts to regulate environmental damage in South Carolina was a 1726 act that sought to limit obstruction of navigable creeks by cut timber (1726, 519). It is possible that this act was written to address creek damming for millponds in the Piedmont. The same act also banned fish

In the great Pine Forests of the South—gathering crude Turpentine—North Carolina. Copyright 1903 by Underwood & Underwood.

Collecting resin from pine trees in 1903. Scraping the bark to encourage the flow of resin eventually killed the trees. *Courtesy Library of Congress.*

poisoning, a method of harvest that would likely be more common in places where shallow running waters could be dammed.

Another South Carolina act written in 1726 helped the emerging livestock industry by offering bounties for predators (1726, 521). Several aspects of this act give insights into how the royal government initially viewed the actions of different socioeconomic groups, as white persons and the enslaved received bounties for "wolf, tyger and bear" while for Native Americans the bounty was offered "for wolf or tyger…and for each wild cat." This suggests that slaves, at least in the early 1700s, could possess firearms and were involved in hunting. The fact that Native Americans could not get a bounty for bears suggests that this animal was important for other purposes. A subsequent act in 1733 eliminated the distinctions among socioeconomic groups and simply offered bounties to anyone bringing in physical evidence of a killed predator.

Although the history books give many details about human conflict and interaction associated with the deerskin trade, a 1769 South Carolina act showed the various negative ecological interactions set in motion when deer were slaughtered primarily for their hides. A preamble to the act stated that both residents and nonresidents of South Carolina were killing deer and leaving the carcasses for predators; this in turn caused predation on livestock (1769, 988). Attraction of predators was not the only problem, as the act also addressed night hunting with torches, deer population declines, Native American hunting rights, subsistence hunting and trespass. The response of the government to declining deer populations was to restrict the killing of does and fawns between January 1 and July 30; buck hunting was banned from September 1 to the last Friday in October and from March 1 to April 30. This represented one of the first efforts to establish hunting seasons in South Carolina. Enforcement of the hunting season was complex, as numerous groups were excluded: Native Americans if an existing treaty stated this exclusion; enslaved people if commanded to hunt by their owners; and persons hunting deer to provide food for themselves or a family. (A slave hunting without a directive from the slave owner was given lashes.) This act also addressed for the first time in South Carolina the issue of hunting on the free range versus hunting in a fenced enclosure. Night hunting with fire was banned on the free range due to accidental killing of humans and livestock. Night hunting was allowed in an enclosure. Finally, the act attempted to limit hunting by nonresidents via a complicated seven-mile rule: if you were more than seven miles from your residence and wanted to hunt, you had to get the permission of the landowner. Violation of the 1769 act was generally associated with fines, physical punishment or work for the common good—a local magistrate collected or directed the fines. However, there was no one in the field enforcing the law, and thus violations were reported by word of mouth, a procedural flaw that likely allowed the colonists to hunt freely.

The deer preservation act of 1769 was amended in 1789 (1789, 1463) to address further problems with prescribed burning, night hunting with fire, certain administrative procedures and enforcement in the field. Specifically, the act was now made required reading by the militias scattered throughout the state, with the assumption that they would serve as game wardens of a sort.

Following the Revolutionary War and leading up to the Civil War, there is some (but not much) evidence of attempts to regulate fishing and hunting beyond those previously mentioned. Most of these attempts dealt with fish or shellfish. In the early 1800s, fish populations of inland streams were apparently in decline due to millpond dams and other obstructions that stopped fish migration. In response, fish passages around these obstructions were mandated on a river-by-river basis. Subsequent acts banned placing of fish traps in or near the fish passages. And in 1847, the government recognized oyster beds as private property and established fines for individuals harvesting this property (1847, 3024). Two aspects of this act are noteworthy. First, the act established different punishments for whites, free persons of color and enslaved people. It also recognized the right of any individual to catch swimming or floating fish above the oyster beds. The treatment of tideland under the water as private property was later modified when tidelands were considered part of the public trust (see the first chapter).

FISH AND GAME ON THE PLANTATION

As profits from livestock, timber and deerskins declined due to various factors, the economy in coastal South Carolina turned to crops such as indigo and rice, a third wave of development that caused much permanent modification of the coastal landscape. Initially, upland forests were cleared by cutting and burning for production of indigo and dryland rice. However, it was the conversion of lowland forest to rice production that entailed the greatest and longest-lasting impacts.[30] Lowland rice culture first began in the late 1600s and continued to the middle 1700s. It targeted isolated pockets of swamp, of which there were and are many in coastal South Carolina. Enslaved people cleared the trees, and then dams were built to collect water for irrigation. Because the wetland soils were rich in carbon and nutrients, rice yields were substantial, and most of the crop was exported from Charles Town. In the mid-1700s, when the enslaved population increased substantially, rice production shifted to swamps bordering coastal tidal rivers.

The conversion of tidal freshwater swamps to rice fields involved cutting massive cypress and tupelo trees, removing or burning the stumps, digging ditches and canals and constructing dikes, a process described in detail by

Wooden barge used to transport rice on the Waccamaw River and then later to transport hunting parties originating at Hobcaw Barony. *Courtesy the Belle W. Baruch Foundation, Hobcaw Barony.*

Heyward. Water or dewatering of the rice crop occurred passively and was controlled by wood structures called trunks built into the dikes. On a rising tide, trunks could be opened and the fields flooded. Subsequently, trunks could be closed, thus holding the water on the fields. On a falling tide, trunks could be opened and the fields dewatered. Extensive areas of tidal swamp were gradually converted to a patchwork of field, ditch and dike. Prior to the Civil War, rice generated great wealth and allowed the emergence of a plantation culture, with Georgetown County at the epicenter.

Leading up to the Civil War, enslaved people composed much of the human population in some coastal South Carolina counties, and most of them lived on rice plantations. As such, the fishing and hunting behaviors of slaves becomes important in understanding local harvest pressures on wildlife in coastal South Carolina and how such pressures were regulated. Because the written record regarding the lives of the enslaved is sparse, archaeologists rely on artifacts, and in the case of fishing and hunting behavior, buried bones around slave quarters can be useful.

The diet of slaves was dominated by foods raised on the plantation and provided as rations: chickens, corn, cows, geese, peas, potatoes and rice. Wild game such as clams, crows, fish, foxes, hawks, opossums, oysters, raccoons, squirrels and turtles supplemented the slave diet.[31] Excavated bones near

Left: Water control trunk allowed either passive inflow of water on a rising tide or restriction of water outflow on a falling tide. *Photo by the author.*

Below: Flooded rice field with earthen dikes in foreground and background. The forested area to the left forms the high-ground boundary of the field. *Courtesy Library of Congress.*

relic slave quarters at Richmond Hill Plantation on the Waccamaw River in Georgetown County showed that the slave diet was dominated by domestic animals, while the planter and overseer made use of a wider variety of both domestic and wild animals, including deer, sea trout and sturgeon.[32] Michie concluded that diets of people living on plantations varied depending on the environmental setting and the freedom of slaves to forage beyond the plantation boundaries. In addition to bones, lead shot, percussion caps and gun flints found near slave quarters suggested that slaves owned firearms and were likely encouraged to supplement their diets by hunting.[33] Considering that slave populations on typical coastal South Carolina plantations numbered in the hundreds, it is easy to envision zones of fish and game depletion in or around the plantations; however, data on this do not exist.

Hunting was also a part of slave work. Bobolinks (rice birds) arrived seasonally in great numbers at the rice fields and consumed much of the crop. Slaves were posted as bird-minders to either shoot them or scare them away with shotguns.[34] Likewise, every plantation had a duck hunter whose task was to kill as many ducks as possible using heavy muskets or shotguns. In the mid-1700s, ducks were apparently so numerous at the time of rice harvest that killing them was more of a necessity than sport.[35] A 1797

Entered according to Act of Congress, in the year 1862, by M. B. BRADY, in the Clerk's Office of the District Court of the District of Columbia.

African American slave village on a Port Royal plantation in 1862. Large numbers of confined slaves put pressure on fish and wildlife on and in the immediate vicinity of plantations. *Courtesy Library of Congress.*

notebook documenting crop expenses for the Sandy Island Plantation on the Waccamaw River listed gunpowder and shot to keep birds and ducks off the crop.[36]

The proprietary government as early as 1712 limited enslaved people from carrying guns off the plantation unless they were accompanied by a white person or were in possession of a written certificate from the slave owner (1712, 314). South Carolina law in 1819 recognized the legitimate need for slaves to carry and use guns primarily for the purposes previously mentioned: eliminating mischievous birds, hunting game and predator control (1819, 2220). But there were similar restrictions as in 1712. And then during the Civil War in 1865, South Carolina considered it a misdemeanor for persons of color to possess military weapons. These same persons were allowed to keep shotguns or rifles used in hunting (1865, XIII). The various acts and laws passed through time in South Carolina indicate dual and sometimes competing goals of prevailing governments: restricting gun possession by slaves while at the same time allowing them to possess guns for utilitarian purposes.

Chapter 4

Up to the Civil War

THE PLANTER/SPORTSMAN

In coastal South Carolina, the time leading up to the Civil War was characterized by little or no fish and game regulation. The few statutes in existence were not generally enforced in a cultural landscape focused on deerskins, timber, livestock and agriculture. Regulatory actions taken by the various governments were more focused on protection of livestock and humans than on fish and game. In addition, much of the rural land was still relatively open, free range and was treated as a commons with no clear responsibility for maintaining the commons. Even recreational outdoor sports were not yet fully developed in the minds of most South Carolinians, as fishing and hunting were primarily for food and not for pleasure. Widespread recreational fishing and hunting did not become popular until after the Civil War.[37]

A very few wealthy planters and businessmen living on the South Carolina coast prior to the Civil War, however, did pursue recreational fishing and hunting. These individuals were broadly educated, well connected and had traveled to Europe, where hunting was highly ritualized and practiced only by the aristocracy. Their memoirs revealed a desire to transfer some of these rituals to South Carolina, along with the codes of proper hunting conduct. The narratives of J. Motte Alston, a planter during the mid-1800s, described in detail the fishing and hunting he experienced in the swamps near the Waccamaw River:

There is a tradition that a gentlemen on Peedee killed 100 ducks by two discharges of a doubled gun i.e., four shots. My brother John brought True Blue eighty ducks by the same number of shots, and visiting the pond next day he found about twenty more.[38]

Among the emerging planter/sportsmen, just like among the hunting aristocracy of Europe, there was an appreciation of guns and gun skills. Wildlife species were understood not just for their food qualities but also in terms of natural history. Unfortunately, game management as practiced in Europe did not initially transfer well to South Carolina because the ecological and agricultural systems were different. Planters modeled the structure of their plantations after English estates, but their land management was fully focused on generating commodities, not hunting experiences. By the mid-1800s, there was agreement that fish and game populations in coastal South Carolina were depleted or were on the decline. The causes were clear: habitat destruction, market hunting and waste. There was naïve hope that recreational hunting by well-informed individuals could fix some of these problems, but there was also hesitancy to limit human enterprise and private property rights in South Carolina to the benefit of fish and game. William Elliott, a successful planter, politician and sportsman from Beaufort who had traveled widely, summarized his thoughts on hunting in 1846:

Thus thinking of the value of amusement in general, and of hunting in particular, I cannot but perceive with regret, that there are causes in operation which have destroyed, and are yet destroying, the game to that extent, that, in another generation, this manly pastime will no longer be within our reach. Sportsman as I am, I am not one of those who regret the destruction of the forests, when the subsistence of man is the purpose. It is the order of events, that the hunter should give place to the husbandman; and I do not complain of it. It is the wanton, the uncalled-for destruction of forests and of game, that I reprehend.[39]

Elliott, like most observers of wildlife in the 1800s, recognized a changed landscape in coastal South Carolina due to human settlement. This perception was aided by a relatively short history spanning the time from first European contact with Native Americans up to the Civil War. Although there were few written descriptions of ecological change, there was and is an abundance of narratives and the telling of stories in South Carolina. Through time, these produced a somewhat mythical version of the original land that eventually became South Carolina: a pristine ecosystem of abundant and limitless natural resources. Placed in a culture initiated by the singular goal of extracting natural resources for subsistence and trade,[40] it is easy to understand how the planter/sportsman came to view unlimited harvest of wildlife simply as a characteristic of life near the tidelands, swamps and rivers of coastal South Carolina. J. Motte Alston provided his perception of the place where he owned a plantation:

> *All Saints Parish, Waccamaw…is a neck of land some three miles wide with the ocean on the east and river on the west; the latter runs parallel to the former. From its position one can readily imagine what an abundant country it was; game of all kinds, deer, wild turkeys, ducks, etc., salt and fresh water, and all that the sea shore afforded.*[41]

But William Elliott described how the landscape he once knew had changed dramatically to the detriment of deer hunting:

> *The uncleared lands, too, bordering on the cultivated portions of the country, are much less densely covered with undergrowth than formerly. The contrast is so striking, the change undergone within the last twenty years so very apparent.…It is mainly to be ascribed to the rearing of increased numbers of cattle…but, above all, by the practice of burning the woods in spring, to give these cattle more luxuriant pasturage.*[42]

And Duncan Heyward began his memoir as follows:

> *In the years now long past, there was no better or more varied hunting to be had anywhere than on the rice plantations along the Combahee, and even today, where these lands have been protected, some game still remains.*[43]

While the planter/sportsman often described the depletion of wildlife in the pre–Civil War South Carolina landscape, the issue was generally placed in the context of rights and responsibilities associated with two groups of people: landholders and others. The "others" category included market hunters, poor people and nonresidents. Enslaved people, at least prior to the Civil War, were not generally included among "others," as they were often deeply involved in the sport fishing and hunting of the planters or they were given tasks that involved hunting to protect crops and livestock. With declining wildlife and thus declining hunting opportunities

13751—Hoeing Rice, South Carolina, U. S, A.

Tideland rice cultivation was not amenable to mechanization, and so even into the early 1900s, the field work was done by hand. *Courtesy Library of Congress.*

for everyone, the planters became more protective of their lands. They attempted to thread a needle with individual strands that recognized universal hunting rights and the tendency of hunters to overharvest but also ensured restrictions on trespass. By the mid-1800s, the colonial commons as described by Greer, had been replaced by the plantation commons (i.e., privately owned estates used by the landowner, the overseers, guests and the resident enslaved).

William Elliott's 1859 essay entitled "Random Thoughts on Hunting" perfectly framed the cultural and regulatory forces conspiring to produce few fish and game laws prior to the Civil War. He also outlined the problems. On the one hand, there were immigrants who had experienced highly restrictive game laws in Europe:

> *The preservation of game is thus associated, in the popular mind, with ideas of aristocracy—peculiar privileges to the rich, and oppression toward the poor. What wonder then, that men...seem bent on the extermination of game.*[44]

And once escaping the tyranny of English game laws, the people of South Carolina assumed a general right to hunt:

> *The right to hunt wild animals is held by the great body of the people, whether landholders or otherwise, as one of their franchises, which they will indulge in at discretion.*[45]

But Elliott himself experienced conflict when the colonial commons overlapped with the plantation commons—more specifically, when he attempted to declare his plantation a preserve for his own hunting:

> *The writer of these pages, finding that during his absence from his property, his game had been destroyed, and his interests, in other respects, sacrificed to this propensity of his overseer.*[46]

Elliott identified "the unrestricted in the neighborhood" as among those who poached his game. But instead of blaming people, he seemed to suggest that common law was at the root of the problem. The law allowed free-ranging livestock to damage unfenced private property; the law was soft on fire hunters, trespassers and game chasers; the law tended to view game as a public resource:

> *I think there will be a reform in this matter—not that I shall witness it. It must be the work of time. When the game shall have been so killed off, that the mass of the people shall have no interest in hunting their neighbors' grounds—the law will be reformed.*[47]

Indeed, Elliott was correct about South Carolina game law and time. Only after the Civil War were laws enacted to address some of the long-standing

Duck hunter and his dog on Dean Hall Plantation in Berkeley County about 1900. Wild rice dominates the former rice fields. *Courtesy South Caroliniana Library, University of South Carolina–Columbia.*

issues he described. But in the years leading up to and during the Civil War, South Carolina did manage to regulate other fish and game issues. (Actually, it was regulating social/political issues.) For example, an act passed in 1855 prohibited nonresidents of the state from hunting and fishing. The only exception was if a landowner granted permission to a nonresident (1855, 4228). The impetus for this law was obvious, considering that northerners frequently traveled to South Carolina in search of fishing and hunting opportunities not available in their home states. And toward the end of the Civil War in 1865, persons of color were banned from carrying military-style weapons and thus were not considered part of the militia (1865, XIII). They were allowed to own and carry firearms typically used for hunting.

Chapter 5

New Restrictions, 1870–1900

THE END OF RICE

The period immediately after the Civil War was a time of great social and economic upheaval, locally in coastal South Carolina and generally in the United States. Emancipation eliminated the labor system on rice plantations. This change, coupled with a series of strong hurricanes, gradually eliminated rice production, and most of the plantation estates were abandoned or fell into disrepair. The great economy driven by the growth and exportation of rice—and the owning of enslaved people—collapsed. As plantations ceased operation, crop and livestock production also initially fell, and it is likely that everyone living on the plantation commons relied more on fishing and hunting to provide food (see letters of Heyward as compiled by Cook and others).

The end of the Civil War also marked the beginning of surges in immigration and industrial development primarily in the North but eventually also in the South. Populations of northern cities expanded, and new markets were created for commodities and raw materials. The largely agrarian society that existed prior to the Civil War was gradually replaced by one in which people lived in cities and worked in industry.[48] With industry also came an increased ability to modify the environment as rivers were dammed, wetlands were filled and new pollution streams were created.

Coastal South Carolina was not well positioned to participate in the Industrial Revolution, a situation that continues to the present. The once-wealthy planters, importers and exporters and the never-wealthy workers

Even after emancipation, African Americans continued to live in the original slave quarters, such as this house on Hobcaw Barony. Note the fishing net on the left. *Courtesy the Belle W. Baruch Foundation, Hobcaw Barony.*

attempted to make agriculture once again a paying enterprise, but the heydays of rice could not be replicated once the labor system changed and rice production began in the Gulf Coast states. The easy timber was harvested, the trade in animal skins was gone and industry was scattered among a few craftspeople. (Then and now, industry was primarily concentrated farther inland or in the Upstate, where streams could be tapped for hydropower.) As in the past, residents of coastal South Carolina turned to natural capital of the coast (i.e., fish and wildlife) to generate income. Their target markets were local, regional and beyond. However, the population of the state was changed by the influx of immigrants not just from England but from other countries in eastern and western Europe. A nascent conservation movement, the emergence of sport hunting and fishing and firsthand experience of many with wildlife depletion and environmental degradation created a political environment more conducive to regulation.

WATER AND FISH

The establishment of navigable water as a component of the public trust allowed for earlier and more frequent regulation of water pollution, fishing and stream modification as compared to game regulation. Indeed, one of the first environmental regulations in South Carolina concerned navigation in streams and fish poisoning (1726, 519). These early laws, written under the royal governors, were seldom enforced. And so again in the 1870s there were further attempts to stem water pollution and other problems in streams of the Upstate. Later, these acts (1870, 235; 1870, 4; 1871, 397) would apply to waterways at the coast. One problem was the catching of fish with seines, traps, weirs and nets that stretched across the entire width of waterways. One solution was the requirement for their removal during certain days of the week. Another problem was the construction of hydropower dams by manufacturers that blocked fish migration. This problem was resolved by requiring the construction of fish ladders or passageways. Finally, the issue of enforcement was addressed by identifying fish commissioners who would find offenders and then levy fines. Several subsequent amendments and acts focused on the raiding of fish traps and the setting of fish traps in fish passageways. The spate of stream regulation laws in the 1870s reflected the willingness of state government to aggressively protect both water quality and migratory fish populations. However, the limits on fishing methods would later create conflict between fishermen in different parts of the state.

The appointment of fish commissioners in South Carolina (1870, 4) coincided with the appointment of a commissioner of fish and fisheries in Washington, D.C., beginning in 1871. This position was a response to the public perception that food fishes on the East Coast, particularly shad and salmon, were declining.[49] The independent but temporally linked appointments of fish commissioners in South Carolina and Washington, D.C., likely represented one of the first informal state/federal cooperative efforts in fish management.

A subsequent South Carolina act in 1878 revealed the beginning of legislative micromanaging of fish and game at the county level (1878, 373). Fish netting, gigging or trapping in freshwater rivers of certain counties (i.e., Marion, Horry, Darlington, Clarendon, Georgetown and Williamsburg) were banned from April 15 to September 1. It is not clear what fish species was the target of this legislation, but it was likely shad (see subsequent section). The shooting of fish with guns was also banned.

Although previous legislation established the position of fish commissioner, apparently the job was vague. As a result, an 1878 act (1878, 600) charged the governor with appointing an unpaid fish commissioner of the state. This person was given a small budget to propagate native fishes and to introduce fishes from other states and places. The job also required the writing of an

Hoop net deployed in shallow waters of the Waccamaw River near Hobcaw Barony. The lower Waccamaw supported numerous commercial fisheries, including for shad and sturgeon. *Courtesy the Belle W. Baruch Foundation, Hobcaw Barony.*

annual report. It is not by coincidence that South Carolina designated a commissioner in charge of fish introductions in 1878. In that same year, the U.S. Fish Commission began importing carp from Europe and started taking applications from the states. South Carolina was the recipient of eight hundred carp in 1880.[50] These foreign fish were introduced in the hope that they would increase and perhaps provide a new source of food in an environment of dwindling native fish.

Fish and game regulations in South Carolina were always difficult to enforce. Violations were dependent on reporting by the general public to an official, typically located in a population center. The fish commissioner of the state was later charged with appointing two or more fish wardens in each county (1879, 104). This was a significant change in enforcement, as wardens could now be based in places where violations were occurring. Collected fines were used to fund expenses of the wardens.

By the 1880s, many subsistence fishermen and hunters in coastal South Carolina had accelerated the harvest when merchants established both methods and routes of export to northern cities. Market hunting (including fishing) became widespread, and the major exports were ducks, shad, sturgeon, oysters and turtles. As this was one of the few industries at the coast, limits were nonexistent. However, there was a law passed in 1884 that required nonresidents to purchase a license if they were involved in market hunting and fishing (1884, 450). This was a modification of the law passed just prior to the Civil War that banned nonresidents from hunting and fishing in South Carolina (1855, 4228). Clearly, South Carolina viewed natural resources as property of the state, held in public trust for residents. However, it was also clear that nonresidents could participate at cost.

Apparently, there were some areas of coastal South Carolina where illegal shad fishing was so pervasive that a special patrol was approved (1891, 721). This patrol was assigned to the Waccamaw River, Great Pee Dee River and Bull Creek and was authorized to seize boats, nets and tackle; it represented the first effort of South Carolina to apprehend illegal fishermen on the water.

Limitless collecting of oysters and an expanding market for them created two problems. One, natural oyster beds were overharvested. And two, the State of South Carolina saw some potential for farming oysters on submerged land not currently supporting oysters. An act in 1891 (1891, 700) directed the fish commissioner to conduct a survey of natural oyster beds and then identify areas not currently producing oysters that could be leased for farming oysters. This marked the first time when the State of South

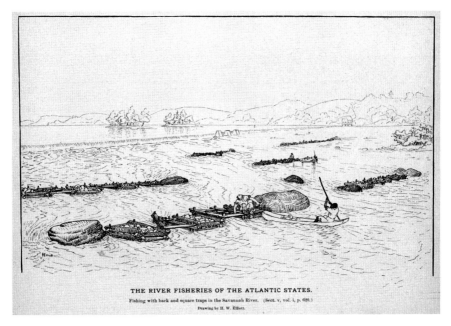

THE RIVER FISHERIES OF THE ATLANTIC STATES.
Fishing with back and square traps in the Savannah River. (Sect. v, vol. i, p. 629.)
Drawing by H. W. Elliott.

An 1880s depiction by H.W. Elliott of wooden fish traps on the Savannah River. *Courtesy National Oceanic and Atmospheric Administration Photo Library.*

Carolina became involved in encouraging private aquaculture on public land. It also marked the first time where a state official governing fish and game was formally directed to cooperate with federal officials.

During this period, essentially all attempts to regulate fish and game harvest focused on methods, seasons, days or licenses. Over time, seasons became more restrictive and licenses more expensive. In 1896, for example, the taking of sturgeon and shad was further regulated by stating that no net could stretch more than halfway across a waterway. The season was further restricted (1896, 102). The wording of state fish and game laws was often vague and provided little guidance for implementation. It was typically up to county commissions to interpret the laws and then determine the best paths for implementation and enforcement.[51]

The close of the period from the end of the Civil War to 1900 was punctuated with an odd South Carolina act attempting to ban hunting, fishing and shooting on Sunday, the Lord's day (1896, 101). Considering the importance of such activities in the culture of coastal South Carolina, it is difficult to envision how this was successfully enforced.

THE SHAD FISHERY

American shad are anadromous fish that spend most of their life in the ocean. After about six years of growth in salt water, they migrate into and then up coastal rivers to spawn. The shad spawning run in South Carolina rivers typically begins in January and continues to April, with February considered the peak month. They do not actively feed during migration but nevertheless can be caught with hook and line; the vast majority of these fish are caught with gill nets and seines.

McPhee considered shad as one of the most important food fish in the United States. Their use by humans can be traced from Native Americans to the colonies to the Revolutionary War and to the present. They were prized for their flesh and roe but, according to Johnson, were clearly overfished. The federal government began informal monitoring of shad populations in 1873. At that time, H.C. Yarrow, working for the federal commissioner, traveled to Savannah, Georgia, and Wilmington, North Carolina, and interviewed fishermen regarding current and historical shad populations in the local coastal rivers. These reports were universally negative, and one statement from a fisherman in Savannah summarized the situation:

> *Mr. J. Higgs, of No. 8 Ellis street, an intelligent fisherman, informed me that it is his belief that there are one-eighth as many shad in the Savannah River at present time as formerly. He attributes the decrease to the numerous traps and nets used since the war, and the offal from gas-works and paper-mills near the City of Savannah.*[52]

The long-term trend for the South Atlantic states, including South Carolina, showed that shad catch peaked in 1897 (Chart 4) and declined through the 1930s.[53] The causes of the shad population decline were always controversial but generally included the damming of rivers, changing markets, pollution and overfishing.

Two rivers in South Carolina historically provided the majority of shad catch: the Edisto and the Waccamaw. The shad fishery on the Waccamaw River in Georgetown County was relatively new but became important to the local economy in Georgetown, particularly in the years following the Civil War, when agricultural exports declined. These fishermen used drifting gill nets and supplied fish locally and to northern markets. Most of the fish were caught near river mouths and thus never had the opportunity to spawn.[54] Tighe wrote about the shad fishing fleet in Georgetown. He estimated that

Right: American shad. *Image created by Duane Raver and courtesy National Fish and Wildlife Service National Digital Library.*

Below: An 1880s depiction by H.W. Elliott of shad fishing on the Edisto River. Note the net stretching from bank to bank and also a rice trunk on the left bank. *Courtesy National Oceanic and Atmospheric Administration Photo Library.*

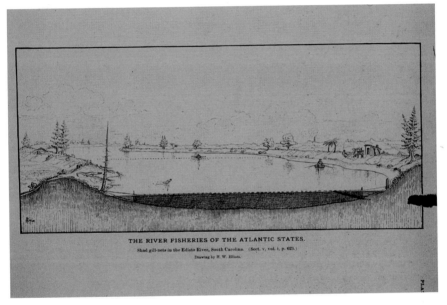

THE RIVER FISHERIES OF THE ATLANTIC STATES.
Shad gill-nets in the Edisto River, South Carolina. (Sect. v, vol. I, p. 623.)
Drawing by H. W. Elliott.

about 150 men were involved, and their catch increased each year from 1883 to 1888 with a peak of about 250,000 fish.[55] This number contrasted with an 1887 report by fish warden R.J. Donaldson, who estimated that 70,000 shad were taken in that year.[56] Donaldson also discussed the public perception that shad were becoming difficult to find. The cause of this decrease was, in his mind, not fishermen but market pressure, primarily from northerners. Fishermen in the Upstate were agitated, as they were under the impression that Georgetown County fishermen or nonresidents in large vessels were illegally fishing the mouths of rivers and thus intercepting most if not all of the migrating fish.[57] To make matters even more confusing, the federal government decided to explore the use of shad stocking in the Upstate to augment declining stocks. This effort was viewed with widespread

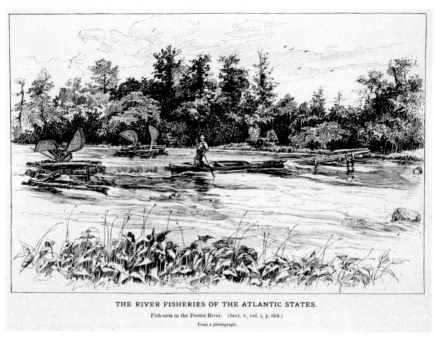

THE RIVER FISHERIES OF THE ATLANTIC STATES.

Fish-nets in the Peedee River. (Sect. v, vol. i, p. 624.)

From a photograph.

An 1880s depiction of rotating shad nets on the Pee Dee River. Note log obstructions to funnel fish into the nets. *Courtesy National Oceanic and Atmospheric Administration Photo Library.*

Large shad ready for market on the Georgetown waterfront. *Courtesy Georgetown County Library.*

Shad Catch in South Carolina

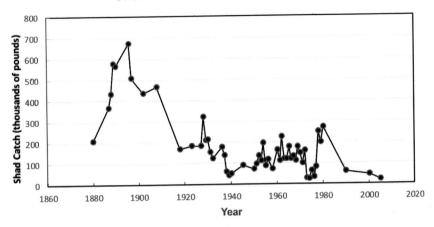

CHART 4. Commercial catch of shad in South Carolina through time. *Drawn from data in Facey and Van Den Avyle.*

skepticism, as positive results were elusive.[58] By the 1960s, shad catch was roughly 20 percent of that in the 1880s.[59]

The controversy regarding South Carolina shad populations in the late 1800s demonstrated the difficultues of tracking and managing a wildlife resource in the near absence of professional staff and field data. Better management would occur later, but only with the emergence of fish and wildlife management as a scientific discipline.

Early in the history of fish and game in coastal South Carolina and to the present, much attention is paid to enforcement activities. Warden Donaldson's 1887 report described in great detail the difficulties of catching and prosecuting shad fishermen in different acts of illegal fishing. His job was made nearly impossible by logistics and the vast areas of water in the different rivers.

THE STURGEON FISHERY

Like shad, sturgeon are anadromous fish that spend most of their adult lives in the ocean. However, it takes six to eighteen years for them to reach maturity, at which point they migrate up coastal rivers and spawn. Sturgeon can reach impressive size, up to eight hundred pounds, and are long-lived if not harvested. All of the major rivers in South Carolina support or can support migrating populations of sturgeon, and they are harvested for their flesh and roe. The sturgeon fishery in South Carolina peaked in about 1890 (see Chart 5) and then collapsed about ten years later.

The Waccamaw River in Georgetown County was historically the center of sturgeon fishing in coastal South Carolina, and there is evidence that sturgeon were a component of the plantation diet in the early 1800s.[60] The nature and extent of sturgeon fishing were initially different than the shad fishery, as it was apparently dominated by nonresidents. In his 1887 report, Donaldson described sturgeon fishing in Georgetown:

> *The fishing was introduced and conducted by Northern men, who came here in January and fished to April. Before the enforcement of the fishing law thousands of these valuable fish were taken by these fishing companies. These men…contributed nothing to the wealth of the state.*[61]

Goode provided more detail of the sturgeon fishery near Winyah Bay:

> *The men live in camps on the river bank, and when fish become scarce in one stream they move to another. The principal sturgeon rivers are the Satilla, Altamaha, Ogeechee, Savannah, and Combahee, in Georgia, and the Edisto and Waccamaw in South Carolina. The outfits are usually owned by capitalists who hire their crews at from $25 to $40 per month.*[62]

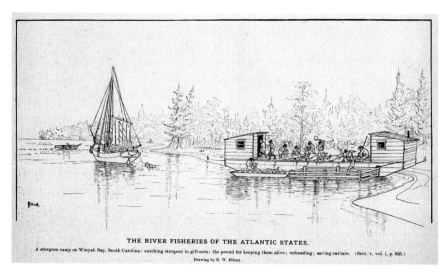

1880s depiction by H.W. Elliott of a sturgeon camp on Winyah Bay near Georgetown. Note the holding pen for live fish. *Courtesy National Oceanic and Atmospheric Administration Photo Library.*

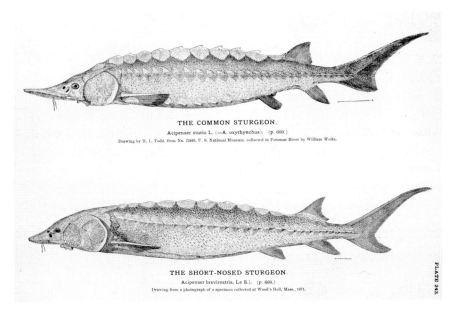

THE COMMON STURGEON.
Acipenser sturio L. (=A. oxyrhynchus). (p. 660.)
Drawing by H. L. Todd, from No. 22495, U. S. National Museum, collected in Potomac River by William Woltz.

THE SHORT-NOSED STURGEON.
Acipenser brevirostris, Le S.). (p. 660.)
Drawing from a photograph of a specimen collected at Wood's Holl, Mass., 1871.

PLATE 243.

Atlantic and shortnose sturgeon. Both species were likely in the coastal South Carolina sturgeon catch. *Courtesy National Oceanic and Atmospheric Administration Photo Library.*

Men holding up a large sturgeon. Sturgeon populations collapsed at the turn of the century due to overfishing and reduced spawning. *Courtesy Georgetown County Library.*

The take of sturgeon was apparently substantial, and the butchering of the huge carcasses on land near the city of Georgetown created an environmental problem so offensive that a city ordinance limiting this activity was passed.[63] According to Goode's report in 1887 sturgeon and shad were packed in Georgetown and shipped to Charleston and then to northern cities. Because the sturgeon fishery on the Waccamaw River involved nonresidents and large vessels, a public perception emerged that sturgeon nets stretching across the mouth of the Waccamaw River negatively affected sturgeon as well as other fish species:

> *We catch drum and bass fish, weighing from 15 to 60 lbs each...though they are not as numerous as formerly, as we believe the sturgeon's nets now used keep them (the fish) back over the bar; and we do urge the Legislature to limit the time of using nets in Winyah Bay from April 1st to Dec. 1st.[64]*

The previous editorial gives a glimpse of the shift in public opinion toward fish and game regulation that existed in 1885 relative to the situation prior to the Civil War. However, simply limiting the season of catch and regulating the stretch of nets were not enough to stop the collapse of the fishery. By 1902, the sturgeon catch was about 20 percent of that in 1897.

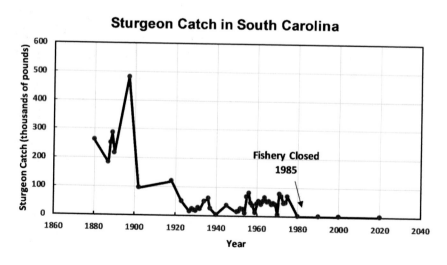

CHART 5. Commercial catch of sturgeon in South Carolina through time. *Drawn from data compiled by Gilbert.*

THE BLACK DRUM FISHERY

Black drum are found in nearshore environments and estuaries along the Atlantic and Gulf coasts. They are bottom feeders, and adults consume mollusks, crabs and shrimp. The name comes from a characteristic drumming sound made when muscles vibrate against the swim bladder. They move to shallow areas for spawing in early spring. Adults can reach up to one hundred pounds.

A famous fishery for black drum in the Broad River emerged prior to Civil War and continued to the 1880s. Elliott described the spectacle of drum fishing in detail:

> *I have taken one which measured four feet six inches in length and weighed eighty-five pounds. Out of twenty taken by me on a particular day, during the present season (April), there were three weighing from sixty-five to seventy pounds each. The smaller-sized fish are excellent for table use—their roes, especially, are a great delicacy; the larger are only valuable when*

Large black drum, likely taken from the Broad River near Beaufort. *Courtesy Beaufort County Library.*

salted and cured like cod-fish, from which when dressed they are scarcely distinguishable in flavor. The planters of this vicinity are skillful fishermen and much devoted to the sport. They succeeded in taking, during the last season, at least twelve thousand of these fish; and when I add, that except the small number consumed in their families, the remainder were salted and distributed among their slaves, not in lieu of, but in addition to their ordinary subsistence, you will perceive that this is a case wherein the love of sport, and the practice of charity, are singularly coincident.[65]

Following the Civil War, drum fishing in the Broad River shifted in purpose:

Since the war the fishery has passed largely into the hands of the negroes, who bring most of their fish fresh to Beaufort and sell them to the dealers or residents of the village at from 25 cents to $1 apiece.[66]

The case of black drum in the Broad River demonstrates clearly how use of a natural resource changed in response to collapse of the plantation culture.

TERRAPIN FISHING

The diamondback terrapin is a relatively small (less than six inches) reptile that lives in salt and brackish marshes of the Atlantic and Gulf coasts. At low tide, terrapins are found buried in the mud; at high tide, they swim through the water in search of snails, crabs and worms. Although relatively small, their meat is desirable.[67] They were heavily harvested in the late 1800s, but declining populations eventually made terrapin harvesting not economically viable.

It is difficult to assess the historical value and extent of the terrapin market in coastal South Carolina:

Just when and where the terrapin fisheries of this district were inaugurated we have been unable to learn, but prior to the rebellion a large number of men engaged regularly in the fishery, and several thousand dozen were shipped annually to the Northern markets, the fishermen receiving an average of $6 per dozen for their catch. It is said that the fishery was at its height, both as to number of men employed and capital invested, in 1860.

Diamondback terrapin. *Photo by Eileen Hornbaker and courtesy U.S. Fish and Wild Service National Digital Library.*

At that time a few Northern fishermen visited the region in small sloops, and parties from Charleston and Savannah had vessels and boats for the same purpose. During the war the fishery was wholly discontinued, but in 1866 it was again pushed with a good deal of vigor, and from 5,000 to 6,000 dozen terrapin were caught between April and November. One vessel with six men landed 870 dozen.[68]

By 1880, methods of catching terrapin in large numbers had apparently become well developed:

Terrapin have been and are still quite abundant in most of the sounds and tide-creeks of the district, but are said to be most numerous in Bull's Bay, and in Saint Helena and Saint Andrew's Sounds. They are usually caught in haul-seines 60 to 90 fathoms long, and 18 to 20 feet deep. The vessel, with a crew of three to six men and one or two boats and seines, enters the larger sounds, and the fishermen visit the little creeks in their bateaux in search of the terrapin.[69]

State legislators perceived a high value in the trade because they required exporters to purchase an expensive license beginning in 1896 (1896, 103). Diamondback terrapins were never abundant—their habitat was restricted, they have low reproductive potential and juveniles and eggs are consumed by numerous predators.[70] As such, it is not difficult to understand how even low levels of harvest could cause rapid population decline. Indeed, such a decline occurred in the late 1800s, and the U.S. Bureau of Fisheries began research to determine best practices for cultivating diamondback terrapins. By 1913, the bureau was offering guidance to residents regarding terrapin breeding and rearing.[71]

THE CHARLESTON COMMERCIAL FISHERY

Large-scale commercial fishing in coastal South Carolina occurred first in Charleston and then eventually in other port cities. Charleston was a population center from the very beginning of colonization, and the shipping port was well developed and maintained. The city was also located close to the ocean and a good harbor, so it is not surprising that industries based on marine resources emerged. By 1880, Charleston had become the largest commerical fish producer on the East Coast.[72] Prior to the Civil War, the first commercial marine industry in Charleston was not locally generated:

> For many years prior to the rebellion the fisheries were controlled largely by Northern fishermen, together with Spaniards, free negroes and a few others who bought their time from their masters. At that time the vessel fisheries were very extensive, and a greater part of the supply was landed by the smacks. In 1860, according to Mr. J.S. Terry, the oldest fish dealer of the city, there were about fifteen New England smacks engaged in fishing for the Charleston market during the winter months. These came South in the early fall and remained till the middle or last of May. They engaged chiefly in the capture of blackfish (Serranus atrarius) and landed enormous quantities, it being not an un common sight to see 100,000 in the cars of the dealers at one time.[73]

As with many commerical enterprises in coastal South Carolina, the Civil War marked a point of social and economic inflection. Emancipated slaves seeking better lives moved from rural areas to Charleston, and many took up

Commercial fishermen on the Georgetown waterfront. The majority of the commercial catch was sold to local markets. *Courtesy Georgetown County Library.*

commerical fishing. This change occurred in concert with the dwindling of the blackfish fishery described earlier. As such, African Americans eagerly stepped into the niche previously occupied by northern fishermen and eventually dominated fishing and fish marketing in Charleston. They used both large and small boats that came to be known as the "Mosquito Fleet." They deployed nets and hand lines:

> *Finding their earnings equal to those of any other class, and the work usually lighter, the number of fishermen has gradually increased until in 1880 there were nearly 600 people either catching or handling fish during some portion of the year, with about 1,700 people depending upon them for support. Of this entire number, 94 per cent are negroes, about 4 per cent. are Spaniards, and only 2 per cent are Americans.*[74]

African Americans in Charleston also controlled marketing and distribution of the catch:

Fishing with a large net on the beach near Pawleys Island in the early 1900s. The catch was sold in local markets. *Courtesy Georgetown County Library.*

The fish dealers of the city, however, control but a small part of the retail trade, for the bulk of the catch is taken directly to the consumer by negroes, who go about the city with trays of fish and shrimp upon their heads.[75]

Enslaved African Americans were involved in many aspects of fishing on the plantation. Their approaches meshed what they brought from Africa and the Caribbean with what they learned from Native Americans.[76] As early as the 1700s, "fishing negroes" were recognized as a special class of highly skilled slaves. Harris as well as Wood described in detail how enslaved and freedmen took fishing skills developed on the plantations and then shrewdly parlayed them into a wide-ranging and successful private enterprise.

THE OYSTER FISHERY

In the years prior to the development of the coastal South Carolina commercial oyster fishery, there were numerous examples of people exploiting this abundant and readily harvested resource. Native Americans, including prehistoric ones, made use of oysters for food, construction and tools. The colonists recognized the potential value of oysters and focused much attention on acquiring grants of land that included oyster beds. Oysters were a staple of the plantation diet. As with several other natural resources such as shad, sturgeon and terrapins, the period after the Civil War was the time when oysters were first commercially exploited on a large scale.

An extensive historical review of the oyster industry in South Carolina was compiled by Burrell. He identified the period from the end of the Civil War to 1900 as an important formative time for the industry. Specifically, restaurants in Charleston started regularly selling oysters to customers, and oysters were delivered to homes with the help of ice. Oyster shell was regularly used to pave roads. As oysters became more popular, shucking houses were built between Charleston and Little River; these oysters were either consumed locally or exported to Savannah and other large cities. The problem of shipping a labile product was soon solved with the advent of oyster canning in the late 1800s. The first canneries were in Beaufort, Charleston and Murrells Inlet. At about the same time canneries were

Collecting seed oysters for an oyster planting project near Beaufort. *Courtesy South Caroliniana Library, University of South Carolina–Columbia.*

Seeding oysters in a tidal creek near Beaufort, site of one of the first oyster canneries in the state. *Courtesy South Caroliniana Library, University of South Carolina–Columbia.*

Women and children working in an oyster shucking facility near Blufton, circa 1913. *Courtesy Library of Congress.*

developing, the State of South Carolina passed an act to encourage the leasing of state lands for oyster cultivation (1891, 700) and then in 1896 (1896, 103) required purchase of a license to sell oysters outside the state. It is unknown if this was a response to depletion of existing oyster beds or if the state was simply attempting to facilitate the growth of an industry. The leasing of state land for oyster cultivation continued into the 1950s. Annual oyster production in South Carolina peaked at about 3 million bushels at the turn of the century. The trend from that point in time forward was marked by declines due to war, labor shortages, oyster disease and pollution.[77]

FIELDS, FORESTS, PONDS AND GAME

The year 1872 was a landmark for regulation of game animals. Several important pieces of legislation were passed in a single act (1872, 121). On the surface, this act appeared relatively mundane, as it set hunting seasons for deer and for certain birds: turkey, partridge, dove, woodcock, snipe and pheasant. However, the posession of deer products (meat and skins) was prohibited out of season, as was hunting with dogs, and the selling of these game birds was banned out of season. By virtue of applying hunting seasons, the legislators recognized for the first time the importance of game protections during breeding and reproduction. Harvest limits were not yet a factor in the game management equation. This act, also for the first time, made a clear distinction between bird species later considered game birds versus others.

The other species of birds were or were not given protections in this act based on their life histories. Insect eaters were protected, unless caught in the act of consuming crops. Birds that were known crop pests or ones that preyed on game birds were not protected. The lack of protection for eagles, hawks and owls continued the long-standing assumption that game was primarly limited by predators and not by harvest. Thus, the list of protected birds included:

> *bats, whippoorwills, fly catchers, thrashers, warblers, finches, larks, orioles, nut-hatches, wood-peckers, humming birds, blue birds, and all other species and varieties of land birds, whether great or small, of every description, regarded as harmless in their habits, and whose flesh is unfit for food, including the turkey buzzard.* (1872, 121)

Excluded from the protected list were

the jackdaw, the crow, the crow black bird, the eagle, and all hawks and owls which prey upon other birds. (1872, 121)

Subsequent 1896 amendments to the act of 1872 began a process where individual counties were granted exceptions to the general rules. This was particularly common for coastal counties and game seasons. The assumption here is that some legislators argued that unique ecological conditions at the coast warranted unique game seasons.

Aquacultue began to emerge in the late 1800s as wild populations of fish and game dwindled. The same act that protected certain useful birds (1872, 121) also established fines for stealing fish or oysters from artificial ponds. And it included, as in previous acts, a ban on fish poisoning. However, in this act, fresh water trout in the Upstate were specifically targeted, and the act of catching them with "poisons or deleterious substances" was associated with a fine (1872, 121).

A long-standing issue affecting hunting in coastal South Carolina and the state was the general perception that private land represented free range for livestock. The roots of this stretched back to the time when both Native Americans and colonists viewed South Carolina as a grazing commons. However, as the population increased, free-ranging livestock were associated with numerous land use conflicts: destruction of crops, accidental shootings, damaging wildlfires set to improve forage and elimination of wildlife habitat. In response, an 1881 act (1881, 472) set out to develop for the first time a general stock law. This act made it unlawful for livestock owners to let their animals run free, with the assumption that the owners would build fences, sometimes at great expense. The act was predicated on counties first building fences on county boundaries unless the boundaries were formed by streams or rivers. If wandering livestock caused damages, the livestock owner was liable, and livestock could be seized (1881, 472). The passing of a "general stock law" marked the end of an era in South Carolina where much of the land was considered free range. As a consquence, hunting and fishing also eventually changed, as new laws were passed to prevent trespass and landowners moved to develop private hunting lands or hunt clubs. These subsequent laws were more wide ranging and more restrictive than the first trespass for hunting law enacted in South Carolina (1769, 988).

THE LACEY ACT: A GAME CHANGER

The Lacey Act of 1900 (1900, 522) represented the first time the federal government assumed control of certain wildlife resources. The writing, editing and eventual passage of this act was influenced by numerous interest groups and by certain wildlife issues that were not being addressed at the state level. This act came too late for species such as the buffalo, passenger pigeon and Carolina parakeet, all driven to extinction or near extinction by market hunting and habitat destruction. An emerging women's fashion trend in the 1880s that used feathers and plumes of birds to adorn hats was threatening songbirds and particularly wading birds such as egrets. At the height of this trend, it was estimated that nearly 5 million birds were killed annually to supply what was known as the millinery trade.[78] Although there were wildlife protection laws on the books, poor enforcement of existing state laws was a problem in South Carolina and nationwide. In final form, the Lacey Act addressed two critical issues: interstate traffic in illegally acquired wildlife and the killing of birds for their feathers.[79] It also provided for federal aid to restore depleted fish and game populations. The passing of the Lacey Act was facilitated by two seemingly different interest groups: sport hunters and conservationists.

Woman wearing a "chanticleer" hat of bird feathers, circa 1912. Market hunting of birds to supply the millinery trade resulted in the wildlife conservation movement. *Courtesy Library of Congress, Prints & Photographs Division.*

In the years following the Civil War, sport hunting was a relatively new pastime. Prior to the Civil War, hunting and fishing were broadly pursued to put food on the table, to generate marketable products or to eliminate predators that interfered with agriculture. There were a few wealthy planters in South Carolina who early on touted the idea of sport hunting (see the fourth chapter), but they were not by any means a large group. Sport hunting gained momentum after the Civil War, first in the Northeast with the publication of magazines such as the *American Sportsman, Forest and Stream* and

THE CRUELTIES OF FASHION.—"FINE FEATHERS MAKE FINE BIRDS."
SEE PAGE 182.

An 1883 *Frank Leslie's Illustrated Newspaper* depiction of bird hunting to supply the millinery trade. *Courtesy Library of Congress.*

American Angler.[80] The writing in these publications helped to clarify the basic tenets of the sport: wise use of the resource, fair methods of take, bag limits, nature appreciaton and camaraderie among sportsmen. A stance also emerged that hunting solely for the pot or market was the root of much game depletion. Sport hunters and conservationists alike looked to state and federal governments for solutions. However, in some instances they took matters in their own hands when it appeared that laws were being ignored. The Palmetto Gun Club in Charleston offered rewards for information about people who violated game and fish laws.[81]

Top to bottom: Great egret, snowy egret and great blue heron. Wading birds like these were subject to intense market hunting during the late 1800s and early 1900s to supply plumes and feathers for the millinery trade. *Photo by the author.*

Chapter 6

Enforcing Fish and Game Laws,
1900–1910

RESOLUTIONS AND ACTS

Following the passage of the Lacey Act in 1900, South Carolina legislators attempted to address the one problem plaguing all previous efforts to protect fish and game: enforcement. As the weight of evidence regarding widespread market hunting and fishing accumulated and public opinion called for action, a 1905 act (1905, 489) established game wardens for the first time. The act stipulated that the governor would appoint one warden per county who was responsible for enforcing all laws protecting, game, game birds and insectivorous birds. It was not stipulated at that time how the wardens were funded. All wild birds were declared property of the state (1905, 474). In the following year (1906, 54), an act was passed to regulate the sale of partridge and quail, to ban the taking of Mongolian pheasants and to require nonresidents to purchase hunting licenses. Fees and fines collected as a result of this act were to be used by the game wardens for enforcement activities. With these two acts (1905, 489; 1906, 54), there was now, in theory, a rudimentary system of game law enforcement in every South Carolina county.

As with game, existing laws protecting the taking and sale of oysters, terrapin, clams, shad and sturgeon were lightly enforced. A 1906 act (1906, 60) attempted to close numerous loopholes. First, the state clarified its ownership of the beds of bays, rivers, creeks and shores of the sea unless conveyed by special grant. These areas, as property of the state, were

Bag limits on ducks at the turn of the century were generous and rarely enforced, as indicated by these hunters in Georgetown. *Courtesy Georgetown County Library.*

held in public trust, to be used for fishing, hunting and shellfish collecting. Because of problems in enforcement of laws, the act stopped further granting of oyster beds by the Sinking Fund Commission. And finally, the act set a process for appointing a Board of Fisheries that would develop and enforce all laws relating to the catching and cultivating of oysters, fish, crabs and terrapin. In contrast to game wardens, board members were paid a stipend. They were also charged to collect taxes on products (e.g., canned oysters) and fees for licenses that could be used to support board activities. The appointment and charge of the Board of Fisheries generally but not specifically separated management of organisms in salt and tidal waters from management of organisms in fresh and nontidal waters, a split that would persist for many years.

While the identification of game wardens in each county was a major step forward in the process of game law enforcement, there was no clear structure for oversight or coordination. The legislature attempted to address this issue by first incorporating the Audubon Society of South Carolina and then charging the society with oversight of game laws and wardens (1907, 315). The charge included regulating interstate commerce in birds, selling

Fish house on the waterfront in Georgetown. *Courtesy Georgetown County Library.*

hunting licenses to nonresidents, protecting all wild birds and their eggs and educating the citizens of South Carolina about the value of wildlife. With the repeal of the 1906 act (1906, 54), where nonresident license fees funded the game wardens, the current act funneled money from fees and fines to a Game Protection Fund used for Audubon activities. The final piece of the plan for giving the Audubon Society of South Carolina control of game laws and county wardens occurred in 1910 with an act (1910, 293) designating the position of chief game warden. The person occupying this job was given a salary of $1,900 and a travel budget of $1,000. The Audubon Society recommended a candidate for the chief game warden job, but approval was required by the governor and the state senate. The first chief game warden was James Henry Rice Jr., an ornithologist, avid hunter and executive secretary of the Audubon Society of South Carolina. Rice and the associated county wardens composed what some consider the first wildlife department in the state of South Carolina.

Two other important pieces of legislation were passed in 1910. One new law placed a ban on the taking of female deer and set bag limits for

Fish, game and agricultural products were shipped to Charleston and northern ports with cargo ships like this one docked in Georgetown. *Courtesy Georgetown County Library.*

partridges, dove, woodcock, turkey and deer (1910, 291). Although the bag limits were liberal, this was the first effort to limit the number of animals that could be taken in a single day in South Carolina. A second new law attempted to make a clear distinction between game fish and other species (1910, 294). The list of designated game fish included jackfish or pickerel, pike, black bass or pond trout, striped bass or rock fish, warmouth, red-belly, robin, bream, copper-faced or ball-faced bream, banded bream, yellow-belly perch, sun perch, red-fin trout or yellow perch, rainbow trout, speckled trout, flyer, crappie, rock bass, goggle-eye and white perch (1910, 294). These species could only be taken with hook and line. If accidentally netted, they were to be returned to the water. The act also regulated trespass for fishing from private ponds and from the private land forming the banks of navigable waters.

By 1910, residents of coastal South Carolina were subject to a wide variety of regulations and laws focused on fish, game and wildlife. Within this regulatory arena were hunting and fishing seasons, restrictions on hunting and fishing methods, bans on game commerce, bag limits and stipulations regarding hunting and fishing trespass. At this point in time, however, the regulatory arena, at least for residents, did not include the purchase of licenses. This factor in the management equation was resisted by the general public and would only be a part of the management equation after the scientific discipline of wildlife biology was better developed.

ROLE OF THE AUDUBON SOCIETY

The involvement of the Audubon Society in South Carolina game law enforcement is an interesting case of nongovernment/government interaction. The first state chapter of Audubon arose in Massachusetts in 1896 and was initially focused on convincing women of Boston to eschew clothing adorned with bird feathers. Members of Audubon were primarily bird lovers, and their efforts to save birds from the plume trade were both practical, inspired and

effective. The cause spread quickly to other states, and in 1905, various state groups were united under the National Association of Audubon Societies. Members of Audubon were also well connected in society and in political circles. As one the few conservation organizations at the time, their tireless efforts to change the laws protecting birds were fruitful. Audubon lobbyists were integral to the passing of the Lacey Act (1900, chapter 52) and were also involved in designation of the first federal wildlife refuge at Pelican Island, Florida, in 1903.

The state-level Audubon societies were impatient with the pace of change and the dysfunction of wildlife protection. Their impatience was fueled by books and reports, such as the one produced by Wayne, detailing the widespread harvest, sale and extirpations of many types of birds. They wrote legislation (Audubon Model Law) and then worked in states to get it passed. They mounted educational campaigns

The Audubon Society was influential in getting bird protection laws written and passed in South Carolina. They identified boys with guns, market hunters and pot hunters as the major causes of bird declines. *Courtesy Georgetown County Library.*

and eventually even hired their own wardens to protect bird rookeries. They formed a journal (*Bird Lore*) and wrote editorials. Considering the rapid rise and early political successes of Audubon societies, it is not surprising that state legislatures turned to them when some government form of wildlife protection was needed.

Control of game law in South Carolina by the Audubon Society was apparently facilitated by a similar move in North Carolina. T. Gilbert Pearson, the national Audubon secretary, reported the success in a 1907 issue of *Forest and Stream*:

> *At the last session of the Legislature of South Carolina, Audubon Society of that State was incorporated as the legal State Game Commission. The law is modeled closely after the North Carolina law. The State Audubon Society has absolute authority in the matter of appointing game wardens and all these officials will operate under instructions from the central office in Columbia.*[82]

The South Carolina state Audubon report, written by Audubon secretary James Henry Rice Jr., summarized his efforts in affecting South Carolina fish and game law and the apparent delay in appointing him as chief game warden:

> *The Society drafted bills for the General Assembly, for the purpose of making uniform the bird-protective laws, for protecting game fish, for a resident license, and for the creation of the office of Game Commissioner. A bag limit of twenty-five Partridges (Quail) and twenty-five Doves, twelve Wood cock and two Turkeys, was made law. Cold storage, except in private dwellings, was prohibited under heavy penalty. Buying, as well as selling, game and gamebirds was forbidden. No protection was given to Ducks, and their shipment out of the state was allowed, as well as the shipment of Bobolinks, known locally as "Rice-birds." But the buying and selling of venison were prohibited, for the first time. Berkeley county was exempted from the pro visions of the law, through the work of politicians. Game fish may be taken only with rod and line at all seasons, and sale is not permitted from March to November, unless the party offering them is prepared to prove that said fish were taken with rod and line. The office of Chief Game Warden was created, but the wording of the act prevented the officer from qualifying until the meeting of the Senate in January, 1911. The law puts the nomination in the hands of the Audubon Society, and Secretary Rice was appointed by the Governor on their recommendation. The resident license did not fare so well.*[83]

The Audubon Society of South Carolina was highly credible in terms of conservation. At the time, various fish resources were in decline, and some people even suggested that the state Audubon should get involved in managing fish, as the "fish commission" was not producing results, specifically with declining shad stocks.

> *I believe that the Audubon Society which is for the purpose of conserving the birds more particularly, is along the right lines, and if they were given a freer hand in the fish matters in the lower part of the state the conditions would be entirely changed.*[84]

However, even with some positive public sentiment toward Audubon-led game and fish regulation in South Carolina, the legislature was low on appropriation. A 1911 issue of *Forest and Stream* summarized the situation:

> *South Carolina appropriates nothing for game protection, and the game fund averages about $3,000 only. Satisfaction seems to prevail.*[85]

James Henry Rice Jr., the newly appointed chief game warden who came to the job on recommendation from Audubon, found a difficult situation in Columbia, as money and politics thwarted his efforts to get a resident hunting license on the books and to enforce game laws:

> *The resident hunters' license bill failed of passage by nine votes, and no substitute was offered. The Audubon Society was divorced from connection with enforcing the laws by the act creating a Chief Game Warden, passed at the session of 1910. The Chief Game Warden was given control of the Game Protection Fund, consisting principally of the non-resident license. This has amounted to only about $600 during the present year. This officer was also given entire charge of the warden force; but he was especially barred by statute from creating any debt, and hence could promise to pay only when funds were in the treasury. The effect of all this was to disorganize the warden force effectually, for the time at least, and it will have to be reorganized ab initio. South Carolina has again fallen into the throes of a political upheaval, to which it is periodically subject, and the cause of bird-protection has suffered.*[86]

Considering the tone of Rice's 1911 report, it is not surprising that his time as chief game warden was limited. It was clear that the South Carolina legislature was not interested in passing legislation that would significantly fund enforcement activities. It was also clear that Rice had ruffled a few political feathers while serving as chief game warden due to his relentless pursuit of laws protecting birds. He resigned in 1913, but then there was a controversy about paying his salary for the year 1912. Governor Cole Blease provided his opinion on the matter in a 1913 message:

> *I have nothing in the world against Mr. Rice personally, but the Legislature said last session they did not want him, that they did not want this officer, and that should be a settlement of this matter.*[87]

As soon as Rice resigned, Audubon submitted another name for consideration by Governor Blease. The nominee was Alfred Aldrich Richardson. Again Governor Blease expressed his lack of support for the position of chief game warden, but Richardson was eventually confirmed. James Henry Rice went on to become a field agent for Audubon and was heavily involved in direct protection of birds from poachers. Over time, the role of the South Carolina Audubon Society in oversight of state game laws dwindled, and in 1917, there was a contentious court battle over the role of the Audubon Society in naming candidates for the chief game warden.[88]

WARDENS AND AGENTS IN THE FIELD

Even though the Lacey Act banned interstate commerce in animals and animal parts, an illegal trade continued, as the law was weak and had no formal methods of enforcement. Further, it only applied to game taken in violation of state law, and South Carolina law was similarly weak. It was up to wardens working for the state, the federal government or the Audubon Society to confront, apprehend and then prosecute poachers who trespassed on private land. In coastal South Carolina, reports of flagrant market hunting were common, and in some instances, confrontations between wardens and poachers turned violent. One such confrontation at the Santee Gun Club was described:

> *On being ordered by the Audubon wardens to halt, these men opened fire with high-power rifles, which was vigorously returned. Thereupon Mitchum and Jordan fled through the marsh, took boat and escaped. Mills surrendered.*

Nobody was seriously hurt. A week before this, as I wrote you at the time, Mitchum and Jordan fired upon a warden at Dean Hall, on Cooper river, on the plantation belonging to Mr. R.B. Kittredge, of Carmel, Putman county, New York. The shot penetrated the warden's clothing at several places, but without injuring him.[89]

After resigning from the post of chief game warden, James Henry Rice returned to the field and described his efforts to stop egret hunters in 1912:

Georgetown, South Carolina, and Savannah, Georgia, are respectively headquarters for financing plume-hunters. A notorious illicit whiskey-dealer, or "blind tiger," named Palmer, in Georgetown, sends out the plumers. I have not been able to get anything definite as to Savannah dealers, beyond rumors, but these are singularly persistent.

In Savannah, Georgia, the leading plume-hunter was Ward Allen, who had been indicted in the Georgia courts and heavily fined, most of the fine being suspended during good behavior. So Allen could not stir, and in fact was conspicuously present in Savannah during the entire spring and summer. There are several charges against him in South Carolina, and he is apparently afraid to cross the Savannah River. These men represent the principal destroyers of Herons between North Carolina and Florida.

Political conditions in South Carolina have been, and still are, regrettable; but there has been no attempt to take away protection from non-game birds, and the sentiment of the people is overwhelmingly in favor of more rigid protection.[90]

James Henry Rice also spent time cataloguing the flow of game toward northern markets. His observations on the wharf at Georgetown characterized well the magnitude of the market trade in game.

J. Henry Rice., Jr., secretary of the Audubon Society of South Carolina, writes me that he has seen 5,000 mallards and black ducks brought into Georgetown for shipment to the north in one day. He has seen woodcock hauled to the market in wheelbar rows. A single firm in Georgetown has marketed 240,000 rail birds, and 720,000 bobolinks have been shipped in one season. Verily the markets are in dire straits for game. Notwithstanding the many restrictions on the marketing of native wild game, enormous quantities of game birds are still sold, and the laws protecting them are often violated by unscrupulous dealers.[91]

At the turn of the century, ducks and other game were regularly sold to local and northern markets, as indicated by this cart loaded with birds in Georgetown. *Courtesy Georgetown County Library*.

Because the Lacey Act was weak in terms of enforcement and because there was essentially no state or county warden system in place, flagrant market hunting in coastal South Carolina would continue with few limits until game wardens were hired who could identify violators in the field and then prosecute them.

Chapter 7

County, State and Federal Interaction, 1910–1940

THE EMERGING WARDEN SYSTEM

The new chief game warden, Alfred Aldrich Richardson, took the job in 1913 and was required to produce an annual report. The series of reports up to 1920 dealt mostly with financial details: expenses for salaries, equipment and travel balanced against income from fines and nonresident licenses. The South Carolina game warden system in charge of enforcing all fish and game laws began in 1912 with a balance of $1,956, an amount considered by some as grossly insufficient considering the scope of illegal fish and game harvest.[92] However, the game law enforcement landscape in South Carolina changed significantly in 1915 with passage of legislation requiring hunting licenses for residents (1915, 151). The following year, the state legislature mandated that revenue from hunting licenses and fines be allocated as follows: 50 percent for salaries of wardens, 5 percent for upkeep of the chief warden's office and 45 percent for schools in the counties where the revenue was generated. This allocation, benefiting local schools, was used repeatedly through time to tout social benefits of the game warden system. The extra revenue also allowed the hiring of more game wardens. In 1920, legislation was passed making the chief game warden an elected position rather than one recommended by the Audubon Society (1920, 428). County game wardens were appointed. Alfred Aldrich Richardson was successful in maintaining his job via election, and then he began in 1921 producing

Red drum caught by sport fishermen in the early 1900s from Winyah Bay near Georgetown were exceptional in size relative to modern red drum populations. Forty-pound fish were common. Size limits on red drum were established in 1986 due to declining stocks. *Courtesy Georgetown County Library*.

The red drum sport fishery of Winyah Bay at the turn of the century was approached with rod and reel and apparently also hand line, as shown in this picture. *Courtesy Georgetown County Library*.

annual reports summarizing significant advances and problems with fish and game regulation throughout South Carolina.

Unlike the first chief game warden, James Henry Rice, who was passionately focused on educating people about the benefits of birds and protecting birds, Chief Game Warden Richardson was more politician than conservationist. He understood that game laws and enforcement of game laws were not universally supported in Columbia and that the governor did not approve of the chief game warden position. He also knew that many in Columbia would rather see game law enforcement handled at the county level rather than by a state agency. As such, his reports were generally positive and stressed that the game warden system was totally financed by licenses and fines (i.e., self-sustaining) even after some of the collected monies were sent to local schools. Parts of this original funding model for fish and game protection in South Carolina continue to the present.

One of the first problems Chief Game Warden Richardson identified was the discrepancy in enforcement between Upstate and coastal counties. He asked for more wardens in the coastal counties, where land areas were large, where poachers and pot hunters were active and where travel was difficult. He also repeatedly recommended a complete rewrite of fishing and hunting regulations because he thought the existing ones were useless, unjust and difficult to interpret. (One of the biggest problems with the existing laws was the continuous process of amendment that gave exceptions to individual counties.) And finally, he repeatedly asked the legislators to pass a fishing license law. His recommendation was to combine fishing and hunting into a single license, the argument being that hunters were paying for game and fish protections, but fishermen were not. In 1919, the state legislation passed a law requiring fishing licenses for nonresidents, but participation and enforcement were minor (1919, 174). The same act explicitly addressed the issue of fish poisoning again and this time included an outright ban on the use of dynamite (1919, 174). The dynamite ban gives some insight into the aggressive methods of wildlife harvest used as late as 1919. Richardson's approach to recommending changes to fish and game regulation was one that employed consistent but low-key pressure through time.

Chief Game Warden Richardson was not a trained wildlife biologist, and it is not even clear if he was an avid hunter or fisherman. However, he did have strong opinions on the best approaches for managing fish and game. In 1923, he did not think that bag limits were effective and was convinced that hunters and fishermen generally took as much as they could catch or kill. Instead of bag limits, he recommended shortening of the fishing and hunting

Trapping of furbearing animals such as raccoons at the turn of the century was loosely regulated and apparently successful near Georgetown. *Courtesy Georgetown County Library.*

seasons, as this was easier to enforce. He was also a fan of predator control and encouraged the killing of all animals that preyed on game birds, nests and eggs. These recommendations were formulated at a time when fish and game populations were either decimated or in decline throughout the state.

In 1923 and 1924, Chief Game Warden Richardson began asking for funds to build fish hatcheries and game farms. He was particularly interested in building a fish hatchery in Georgetown that would supply fish to up-county streams. This was clearly an attempt to mediate the long-standing dispute between net fishermen in Winyah Bay and stream fishermen farther inland. The proposed game farm would grow turkeys, pheasants and deer that would be made available to landowners so game populations could be restored.[93]

Chief Game Warden Richardson was mostly confined to an office in Columbia, where he attended meetings and court hearings. However, the wardens in the field did provide him with some valuable information. Apparently, a law protecting does was effective, as wardens reported in

Above: Improved transportation and new types of firearms, such as the automatic shotgun, increased the potential for waterfowl and game bird harvest in coastal South Carolina. *Courtesy Remington Arms Company.*

Opposite: The early 1900s saw advances in both guns and ammunition used for hunting waterfowl on the coast of South Carolina. *Courtesy Remington Arms Company.*

1928 seeing deer where previously there were none.[94] On the other hand, the depletion of game fish from Upstate streams was severe, probably due to pollution, dams and overfishing. Richardson continued to advocate for shorter fishing and hunting seasons, as well as for fish hatcheries to replenish stocks. He educated state legislators about the impacts of new guns, ammunition and transportation methods, all of which increased hunting pressure.

By 1930, Chief Game Warden Richardson had changed his mind regarding the utility of bag limits, at least for fish.[95] He recommended bag limits, size limits and changes in the mesh size of shad nets—all to allow more

fish to be successful at reproduction. In 1931, he was successful in getting the first fish hatchery in Greenville County. This focused on replenishing trout in Upstate streams.

Even with bag limits, licenses, closed seasons and wardens, game continued to decline, leaving the state legislature with only one final option in conservation and restoration of fish and game: sanctuaries. In 1926, it gave authorization to the chief game warden to develop wildlife sanctuaries in cooperation with private landowners:

> [T]*he Chief Game Warden is hereby authorized and directed without any cost whatsoever to the State to designate and establish sanctuaries where game, birds and animals may breed, unmolested: Provided, that if any landowner shall enter into any agreement with the said Chief Game Warden to set aside and turn over to the State for such purpose any certain number of acres of land: Provided, further, that there shall be no hunting or trespassing upon such lands so designated as a sanctuary by anyone, for a period of five years from date of agreement.*[96]

The chief game warden reported in 1933 that 111 tracts of land were under cooperative agreements as sanctuaries and that these tracts totaled 120,175 acres.[97] Although the State of South Carolina did not own these lands, designation of them as sanctuaries represents the start of a trend in wildlife protection that continues to the present.

In 1935, a Game and Fish Commission was established by state law (1935, 336). This group, with members appointed by the governor, comprised

Sharks taken from Winyah Bay near Georgetown in the early 1900s were also exceptional in size relative to modern populations. *Courtesy Georgetown County Library.*

Bream, golden perch, goggle eye (warmouth), mudfish and catfish taken from fresh water near Georgetown in the early 1900s. The same freshwater fish are found there today. *Courtesy Georgetown County Library.*

six members, one from each Congressional district. The purpose of the commission was to review all fish and game laws, to advise the chief game warden and to consider recommendations from the warden. It is difficult to determine if this extra layer of oversight was helpful for the chief game warden, but at least now he had a group of politicians that could potentially act on his ideas for reforming fish and game laws.

Reports of the chief game warden show that from 1912 to 1940, the warden system grew from a handful of wardens collecting $3,790 from licenses and fines to ninety-three wardens collecting $214,289 from licenses and fines. However, by the early 1900s, fish and game regulation and management in South Carolina was not just the business of the state but was also influenced by a series of federal laws acts aimed at conserving and restoring fish and wildlife. The major thrust of these efforts was designation of wildlife refuges, hunting seasons and development of protections for certain animal species harmed by market hunting. Along with these federal programs was the requirement for greater and deeper cooperation between South Carolina Fish and Game and the federal Bureau of Biological Survey.[98]

MIGRATORY BIRD TREATY ACT OF 1918

This Migratory Bird Treaty Act (MBTA) is considered by some as the first serious attempt by the federal government, more specifically by the Bureau of Biological Survey, to stop market hunting and the selling of nongame and game migratory birds or parts of birds, including nests, eggs and feathers. The initial treaty was signed with Great Britain on behalf of Canada. Subsequent treaties were signed with Mexico, Japan and the Soviet Union. The MBTA of 1918 included the following sections that were made more specific through time:

- *Definitions of Migratory Game Birds, Migratory Insectivorous Birds and Other Migratory Nongame Birds*
- *Rules for How Migratory Game Birds May Be Hunted (i.e., gun type, gun gauge, decoys, blinds etc.)*
- *Open Hunting Seasons for Migratory Game Birds*
- *Bag and Possession Limits for Certain Migratory Game Birds*
- *Rules for Shipping and Transporting Certain Migratory Game Birds*
- *Identification of Enforcement Personnel*
- *Permitting*
- *Fines*

A primary goal of the MBTA was to bring some uniformity to the varied state game laws and also to establish a large group of paid enforcement personnel. Lack of enforcement was a major flaw of the Lacey Act in 1900. Enforcement actions taken by federal personnel were regularly publicized. In South Carolina, the first legislative response to the MBTA was a declaration that regulations of the MBTA were indeed regulations of the state. However, state fines for violations were small: not less than ten dollars or more than twenty-five. Challenges to the MBTA generally focused on state versus federal rights in wildlife regulation. Nevertheless, the courts firmly established the valid role of the MBTA in protecting a public resource contributing to food production, recreation and aesthetic enjoyment.[99]

MIGRATORY BIRD CONSERVATION ACT OF 1929

The Migratory Bird Conservation Act (MBCA) authorized the federal government to acquire and protect wetlands serving as refuges for waterfowl. Prioritization of potential projects for purchase or rental was handled by forming a Migratory Bird Conservation Commission, comprising both federal and state personnel. The commission reviewed abundant data collected over a forty-five-year period by the Biological Survey and then made recommendations. The only stipulation for the states was that they must consent by law for the land acquisition by the federal government. As with many acts and regulations focused on wildlife protection, the MBCA was initially without a permanent source of funds. However, stop-gap appropriations and later acts provided means for funding land acquisitions starting in 1929.

One of the first projects in coastal South Carolina targeted by the MBCA was the Cape Romain National Wildlife Refuge, a project of 32,555 acres located between Charleston and the Santee Delta. The 1930 report of the Migratory Bird Conservation Commission outlined the legal issues that had to be overcome to make this project successful.[100] Target conservation species were migratory waterfowl and wading birds. As such, the refuge needed to include vast areas of tideland in the parcel owned by the State of South Carolina. Fortunately, no prior claims to the tidelands were found, and thus the state agreed to turn these waters over to the federal government. Areas above the high tide mark, such as islands and maritime forests, were privately owned; these areas were purchased outright at a cost of seventy-five cents per acre. Within the Cape Romain National Wildlife Refuge were numerous impoundments, legacies of historical agriculture. Impoundment management for waterfowl would later pose both ecological and legal challenges.

Even before the MBCA, the federal Bureau of Biological Survey was active in identifying lands and waters offering unique habitat that might serve as wildlife refuges. In 1927, it was successful in having 2,352 acres on the Savannah River in Jasper County designated as the Savannah Bird

Francis Marion National forest, Cape Romain National Wildlife Refuge and the Intracoastal Waterway at about the time when both the national forest and wildlife refuge were designated. Old impoundments are visible in the background. *Courtesy South Caroliniana Library, University of South Carolina–Columbia.*

Refuge by Executive Order 4626. In 1931, President Herbert Hoover signed another executive order (5748), adding 207 acres and changing the name to the Savannah River Wildlife Refuge. A third executive order (7391), adding 22,870 acres of land and subsequent land additions from the federal government, eventually culminated in a presidential proclamation (2416) naming the refuge the Savannah National Wildlife Refuge in 1940. (Designation of the Savannah National Wildlife Refuge coincided with the formation of the U.S. Fish and Wildlife Service, a federal agency made by combining the Bureau of Biological Survey with the Bureau of Fisheries and placed with the Department of Interior.) Like the Cape Romain National Wildlife Refuge, the Savannah River National Wildlife Refuge included tidelands, islands and historical rice impoundments. The inclusion of historical rice impoundments in these and subsequent coastal South Carolina wildlife refuges suggests a certain bias on the part of fish and wildlife personnel to preserve a type of man-made habitat used by waterfowl and wading birds.

In 1938, an island at the mouth of the Savannah River was designated as the Tybee Island National Wildlife Refuge by Executive Order 7882. Originally a small shoal supporting good migratory bird habitat, it was enlarged when spoil from dredging of the Savannah River was deposited.

MIGRATORY BIRD HUNTING AND CONSERVATION STAMP ACT OF 1934

The Migratory Bird Hunting and Conservation Stamp Act (also known as the Duck Stamp Act) required every waterfowl hunter sixteen years of age or older to purchase a duck stamp at a price of one dollar. Funds generated from this activity were then used to purchase wildlife refuge lands. The program was proposed by Jay N. "Ding" Darling, a cartoonist and prominent conservation activist who headed the Bureau of Biological Survey at the time. Duck stamps represented a unique conservation approach on the part of the federal government in that hunters paid to support the resource on which their sport depended.

Top: The first duck stamp issued under the Migratory Bird Hunting and Conservation Stamp Act of 1934 cost one dollar. Funds were used to support wildlife management and wildlife refuges. *Courtesy U.S. Fish and Wildlife Service Museum/Archives.*

Bottom: By 1955, a federal duck stamp cost two dollars. Hunters signed the stamp and then affixed the stamp to their hunting licenses. In 2020, the stamp cost twenty-five dollars. *Courtesy Phil Wilkinson.*

PITTMAN-ROBERTSON ACT OF 1937

The Pittman-Robertson Act (PRA) established a tax on guns and ammunition. These funds were funneled to states for wildlife protection and habitat management. In contrast to previously passed federal acts, the PRA represented what could be a significant stream of funds flowing to the states and was emblematic of programs enacted under President Roosevelt's New Deal. However, there were also stipulations and conditions that states were required to satisfy before funds could be allocated. Among these requirements were transparency in project details, statements of cooperating agencies and entities, bidding, contracting, project milestone reporting, cost accounting, vouchers, hiring guidelines and delegation of authority—all subject to review by the chief of the Bureau of Biological Survey. The volume of reporting made necessary significant changes in state fish and game departments, including the game warden system existing in South Carolina.

In his 1937 report, Chief Game Warden Richardson laid out the potential impacts of the PRA in South Carolina and then suggested changes to the South Carolina Game and Fish Department necessary to satisfy requirements of the PRA.[101] The 10 percent tax on ammunition and sporting goods was estimated to generate about $45,000 per year. To get these funds, South Carolina needed to ensure that license fees paid by hunters were used solely for support of the South Carolina Game and Fish Department. While this may seem obvious, remember that part of license fees collected were previously diverted to support local schools. The 1937 report also suggested that game wardens be selected by a civil service process. This was a clear federal requirement. Finally, the chief game warden recommended the state be zoned and that suitable fish and game laws be passed relevant to each zone.[102]

HATCHERIES FROM THE FEDERAL GOVERNMENT

By 1940, the South Carolina Game and Fish Department owned twelve fish hatcheries, all of them located in the Midlands or Upstate. Although capable of raising millions of fish for stocking in streams and lakes, these hatcheries were, according to Chief Game Warden Richardson, not operating at full capacity due to lack of state funds. The hatcheries were built through the

Fish hatchery near Matthews constructed via the Work Projects Administration (WPA). *Courtesy South Caroliniana Library, University of South Carolina–Columbia.*

Quail hatchery near Murrells Inlet, South Carolina, constructed via the Work Projects Administration, circa 1930–40. *Courtesy South Caroliniana Library, University of South Carolina–Columbia.*

federal Works Progress Administration (WPA), another New Deal agency, at a cost of about $500,000. The irony of having fully functional fish hatcheries but no operating funds was not lost on Chief Game Warden Richardson when he asked in this 1940 report, "What are you going to do with them?" His recommendation, one repeated in every report, was to implement a statewide fishing license with the revenue used for operating fish hatcheries and stocking streams.[103]

A quail hatchery operating at the same time was faring better. Like the fish hatcheries, the quail hatchery was received from the federal government and produced about five thousand birds per year. Richardson kept the quail hatchery in the black by charging counties for their allotted birds.

SANTEE COOPER LAKES

Following the Civil War, South Carolina went from being one of the richest states to being one of the poorest. Electricity was a luxury available only to those living in the major cities. With the election of President Roosevelt came numerous efforts by the federal government to develop public power generating capacities. The flow of federal grants and loans required a state entity. Thus, the South Carolina Public Service Authority (i.e., Santee Cooper) was formed in 1934. The mission of this state-owned utility focused on generating electricity and improving navigation, but secondary goals included flood control, wetland management, reforestation and eradication of malaria. Although initially blocked by private interests, this state agency cleared all the legal hurdles in 1939 and put in motion the blueprint for a massive hydropower project on the Santee and Cooper Rivers. Although located in the coastal plain roughly sixty miles from the coast, the Santee Cooper Power and Navigation Project had far-reaching impacts on fish and game both locally and at the coast.

In this 1940 report, Chief Game Warden Richardson described a historic meeting in Charleston with delegates from the U.S. Fish and Wildlife Service and Santee Cooper where details for wildlife refuges and wildlife management associated with the Santee Cooper lakes were discussed.[104] The project required clearing about 177,000 acres of forest (most of it swamp), extensive scraping and earth moving, relocation of towns and farms and construction of locks and dams. The entire area of the project was relatively flat, and the rivers were low gradient. There were concerns that

Stumps of trees remaining on land that would eventually be flooded to form the Santee Cooper lakes. *Courtesy Library of Congress.*

fish populations in the new lakes would not reproduce due to dramatic water level fluctuations, and the wildlife migrating out of the flooded areas needed a refuge. Migration of anadromous fish found in the rivers such as blueback herring, shad, sturgeon and striped bass was a real issue but not of major concern at the time of project planning. The solution, at least for fish and wildlife, was to develop fish hatcheries and also to plan both state and federal wildlife refuges adjacent the newly emerging lakes. With some urgency due to World War II, construction started in 1939 and was completed in 1942.

It is difficult now to envision how such a large project was completed in such a short time. A low dam on the Santee River resulted in Lake Marion, with a flooded area of about 110,000 acres. The impounded water of Lake Marion then flowed through a diversion canal to Lake Moultrie (area 60,000 acres). From there, most of the water flowed through a hydropower dam and navigation lock at Pinopolis to the headwaters of the Cooper River and then on to Charleston Harbor.

Major rivers in South Carolina flowing from inland areas to the coast are critical for fish and wildlife, as they lead to historical spawning habitats of

Cut-over land and remains of a farm that would eventually be flooded to form the Santee Cooper lakes. *Courtesy Library of Congress.*

Dam and spillway on Lake Marion, part of the Santee Cooper Hydroelectric and Navigation project located on the Santee River, circa 1940. *Courtesy Boston Public Library.*

certain anadromous fish and set the stage for ecological conditions of estuaries where there is mixing of fresh and salt water. The immediate impact of the Santee Cooper lakes was diversion of nearly all the flow from the Santee River to the Cooper River. As fresh water coming down the Santee River dwindled, sediments that historically formed the Santee Delta decreased and salinity in the estuary at the mouth of the Santee River increased. On the other hand, with more fresh water coming down the Cooper River, sediment loading increased and salinity decreased in Charleston Harbor. There were concomitant changes in ecological communities. For example, increased salinity at the mouth of the Santee River caused expansion of clams and oysters and salt water intruded into the Santee River.[105]

In the years following completion of the Santee Cooper Lakes, numerous unanticipated changes occurred creating both opportunities and problems with fish and wildlife. A migratory population of striped bass became locked in the lakes and initially thrived, creating a successful recreational fishery. Commercial shipping through the lakes did not thrive, but the navigation lock on Lake Moultrie, when opened on a regular basis, provided opportunities for anadromous fish migration. And fish populations resident in the Santee River—including catfish, bass and bream—exploded in the new lakes, characterized by nutrient-rich water and abundant structure composed of standing dead timber. But these positive impacts were overshadowed by the accumulation of sediments in the Cooper River that impeded navigation of military and commercial vessels. The eventual solution to silting problems on the Cooper River involved construction of a canal directing water from Lake Moultrie back to the Santee River (i.e., the Rediversion Canal). Rediversion of water in Lake Moultrie was accomplished in 1985 by building a second dam at St. Stephen. This dam generated power and included a fish lift so partial migration up the Santee River was restored.

Although many of the impacts of constructing the Santee Cooper Lakes are unknown, as little or no ecological monitoring prior to lake construction was done, clearly the project and subsequent modifications caused wide swings in water salinity at the coast, shifts in ecological communities and changes in fish migration, all documented in Hockensmith's 2004 report. However, the refuges associated with the lakes greatly expanded land for public hunting and wildlife protection. The Santee National Wildlife Refuge was formed in 1941–42 primarily to mitigate loss of wildlife habitat as a result of lake construction. Funds were provided by the Migratory Bird Conservation Act. This refuge was initially about 78,369 acres of leased land comprising swamp, impoundments and other habitats on both Lake Moultrie and Lake Marion. But the area of the refuge changed through time due to lease termination, and at present, most of the refuge is associated with Lake Marion.

Chief Game Warden Richardson outlined in his 1941 report some of the complicated negotiations between the State Game and Fish Department (SGFD), the South Carolina Public Service Authority (SCPSA) and the U.S. Fish and Wildlife Service (USFWS)—SCPSA providing $100,000 to USFWS for construction of a fish hatchery and for wildlife plantings, SGFD and USFWS splitting jurisdiction of the lakes, hunting and fishing allowed on the part controlled by SGFD and hunting not allowed on the part controlled by USFWS. In the end, Chief Warden Richardson was positive about the project:

> *When the Santee-Cooper Project was first started, it was believed by many people that wildlife would be destroyed. It now appears, and many of the same people who fought the project on account of wildlife now agree, that on this area and in these two lakes the public of South Carolina will be afforded the best fishing and wildfowl hunting it has ever had.*[106]

THE INTRACOASTAL WATERWAY

Rivers and harbors were integral to settlement and trade patterns in coastal South Carolina starting with Native Americans and continuing to the present. It was not by coincidence that Charleston and Georgetown were major economic centers, as both were located on relatively deep harbors (at least twelve feet for Charleston) that could accommodate large vessels and were also on rivers that allowed movement of goods to points upriver. The importance of rivers in the early commerce of South Carolina was reflected in the high volume of legislation aimed at regulating or eliminating obstructions from navigable waterways. The state often improved navigation by building small canals or locks when falls, rapids or shallow water were present, but these projects were inland and of local utility; a good shipping route from the central parts of the state to Charleston or Georgetown was still lacking in the late 1700s. In 1800, a private investment group completed the Santee and Cooper Canal, a twenty-two-mile ditch connecting the Santee River to the Cooper River. This waterway was built to provide a more direct route for agricultural products produced in the central part of the state to reach Charleston without negotiating the difficult Santee estuary

Dredging the Minim Canal in 1895, a waterway connecting Winyah Bay to the Santee River that would eventually become a part of the Intracoastal Waterway. *Courtesy Georgetown County Library.*

and open ocean. Changing market conditions and railroads eventually led to abandonment of the canal in 1858.[107]

Clearly, the most ambitious and far-reaching navigation improvement project in coastal South Carolina was the Intracoastal Waterway (ICW). It was initially proposed by the U.S. Army Corp of Engineers in 1913 as a single project stretching from Beaufort, North Carolina, to Key West, Florida. The goal was to provide an alternative shipping route for vessels not suited to the open ocean. However, funding and approval for the entire project were elusive, and so it was built in sections over time. The northern section from the Cape Fear River in North Carolina to Winyah Bay in South Carolina was started in 1930 and completed in 1936. Construction throughout South Carolina depended on local conditions. In some areas, the natural waterways were the required depth (four to twelve feet) so that nothing was needed other than channel markers. In other areas, dredging was necessary, and in still other areas of high ground, where no previous waterways existed, canals or cuts were excavated. Spoil material was typically spread adjacent the ICW.

Dredging the Intracoastal Waterway near Georgetown in the early 1900s. *Courtesy Georgetown County Library.*

The middle section from Winyah Bay to Charleston was patched together with a series of projects starting in 1900 and ending in 1936. Subsequent rounds of funding allowed for a progressively deeper channel. The southern leg of the ICW stretching from Charleston to Beaufort was started in 1929, and final deepening occurred in 1940.

Because the ICW has been a feature of the coastal South Carolina landscape for so long, it is difficult to envision the distribution of land and water prior to the ICW without the benefit of historical maps. In situations where rivers and their estuaries were relatively isolated, the ICW clearly forged new connections and allowed new paths of fish exchange. Relatively deep water was made more common. But perhaps more importantly, the ICW increased the volume of water at the coast where fresh and salt water mixed, thus creating a patchwork of habitats: fresh, brackish and salt water. Disposal of dredged or excavated material was always an issue with the ICW during construction and after construction. Disposal sites are typically wetlands where spoil material either forms the basis of a new ecosystem substrate,

Intracoastal Waterway near Little River. Although originally designed for commercial shipping, it is now used primarily for recreational boating and fishing. *Photo by the author.*

smothers the existing biota or washes back into the waterway, where it reduces water quality.[108] In certain situations, spoil disposal contributes positively to habitat, as was the case with Tybee Island National Wildlife Refuge. Over time, the ICW saw less traffic from commercial vessels and more traffic from recreational boaters and fishermen. At present, it is the primary route for pleasure boaters traveling up and down the Atlantic Coast.

CIVILIAN CONSERVATION CORPS AND STATE PARKS

A 1935 act (1935, 113) gave the State Commission of Forestry (established in 1927) the mandate to develop state parks. Up to that point, the work of the commission and State Forester H.A. Smith was primarily focused on studying forest resources of the state that were severely degraded due to overharvest and then pursuing actions to improve forest conditions. These actions typically involved tree planting and fire protection. However, with the new charge, a Division of State Parks was formed. From the beginning, it was understood that state parks were not for tree production but rather for recreation by the people of the state. The value of state parks as wildlife habitat was also explicitly recognized. Construction of the first few state parks was made possible by local land donations and the work of the Civilian Conservation Corps (CCC), deployed at on-site camps. There was also cooperative aid from the National Park Service, the U.S. Forest Service and the various counties. In his 1934 report, State Forester Smith described initial work on two state parks at the coast: 320 acres of land donated by the Myrtle Beach Farms Corporation that would later be Myrtle Beach State Park and 1,300 acres of land donated by the City of Charleston that would later be Edisto River State Park.

The 1935 report of State Forester Smith essentially established the philosophy and goals of the South Carolina State Park system:

> *The State Park System of South Carolina is a part of a National System of State owned and controlled areas dedicated to increasing the interest of the general public in the great outdoors with particular reference to the conservation of forests and wildlife, to providing recreational areas for our people and to the preservation of places of historical interest.*[109]

This multi-use philosophy—including recreation, wildlife and history—was clearly outside the normal realm of the Commission of Forestry but reveals the influence of the National Park Service and the U.S. Forest Service in guiding state park evolution in South Carolina. The establishment of state parks as wildlife sanctuaries with no guns or dogs, but with regulated fishing, was a continuation of a wildlife sanctuary effort started by the state in 1926.

By 1941, with abundant labor from the CCC, cooperation from federal agencies, park revenues and federal aid, there were four coastal state parks: Edisto Beach, Givhans Ferry, Hunting Island and Myrtle Beach. Another park was planned for the shores of the new Santee Cooper Lakes. Across the state, there were 34,753 acres of land in sixteen parks. Four areas within these parks were developed for use by African Americans. However, in 1942, the war effort changed the trajectory of park development. The CCC was redirected to other assignments, and many of the parks served in various war effort capacities. After the war, the state park system continued to develop new models for serving the changing recreational tastes of residents and tourists while at the same generating income. Self-funding became necessary when federal funds dwindled. However, the original concept of state parks as wildlife refuges persisted, thus making the state park system an important piece of the fish and game management puzzle at the coast and statewide.

Atalaya at Huntington Beach State Park in 1962. *Courtesy Open Parks Network.*

Atalaya at Huntington Beach State Park in 2020, showing height growth of dune shrubs and trees due to vegetation protection within state park boundaries. *Photo by the author.*

CIVILIAN CONSERVATION CORPS AND THE FRANCIS MARION NATIONAL FOREST

The Francis Marion National Forest (FMNF) located at and near the central part of the South Carolina coast currently occupies about 260,000 acres. The origin of the FMNF stretches back to 1927, when the U.S. Forest Service was searching for a project on the coast where forest restoration and best land management practices could be demonstrated on a grand scale.[110] Much of the forest in South Carolina at that time was overharvested, poorly managed and fire prone. Furthermore, landscape change was widespread due to conversion of forest land to agriculture and wetland drainage. Meetings between the U.S. Forest Service and the South Carolina Forestry Commission eventually identified a target area in Berkeley and Charleston Counties. Negotiations commenced primarily with large timber companies that owned much of the land in a region that was sparsely populated and

Logging operation using rails to remove large cypress trees from a Georgetown County forest. Timbering at the turn of the century often occurred with little or no reforestation. *Courtesy Georgetown County Library.*

Conversion of forest to agricultural land required ditching and draining. Piles of tree debris in the background suggest that this forest in Georgetown County was logged and then cleared of stumps in the early 1900s. *Courtesy Georgetown County Library*.

The largely forested landscape of coastal South Carolina was changed to a patchwork of forests and fields at the turn of the century. These landscape changes had negative effects on most wildlife populations. Note the forest remnants in the background of this Georgetown County soybean field. *Courtesy Georgetown County Library*.

Turkey taken in 1943 from the specially designated wild turkey management area in the Francis Marion National Forest. *Courtesy U.S. Forest Service.*

economically depressed. The land sale negotiations were protracted but were almost complete by 1935, and President Roosevelt designated the new national forest in 1936.

The hard work of developing the new Francis Marion National Forest was done largely by the CCC, recruited from the nearby African American population.[111] They built roads, fire towers and firebreaks. Forests were restored by preparing sites and planting seedlings. The cooperative management agreement signed by the U.S. Forest Service and South Carolina Fish and Game outlined how the two agencies would operate the new national forest. Some key components of the agreement dealt with the provision of game wardens, the closing of hunting seasons, the remission of funds collected for special licenses, the development of fish and game management plans, fish and game stocking, equipment sharing and funding.[112] Most importantly, the FMNF would serve as an important site for the restoration of deer and turkey populations near the coast.

Chapter 8

Expanding Public Lands, 1940 and Beyond

COORDINATION AND CONTROL

By 1940, there were numerous departments, divisions, boards, commissions and authorities involved in managing the natural resources of South Carolina. Due primarily to abundant New Deal federal aid, most of these entities were heavily involved in purchasing or leasing land for fish, game, navigation, power generation, forestry and agriculture. There was also a growing portfolio of private/state and state/federal cooperative agreements. But in the new economic and political environment after World War II, there was concern about the overall efficiency, cost and outcomes of state efforts to manage natural resources. As a result, a comprehensive study of natural resources administration was completed by Christian Larsen in 1947.

Larsen's study included entities involved in fish and game, forests, minerals, power generation and commercial fisheries. His sweeping report revealed numerous shortcomings in administrative function. Among the three entities directly involved in fish and game—the State Board of Fisheries, the office of the chief game warden and the South Carolina Forestry Commission—he described the following issues:[113]

- *Little integration or coordination.*
- *Variable and inconsistent reporting.*
- *No merit or civil service system for personnel.*
- *Lack of oversight in budgets and purchasing.*
- *No good accounting of federal personnel or aid.*

The review revealed several administration failures. Apparently, the Game and Fish Commission formed in 1935 to advise the chief game warden experienced internal conflict and resignations and then ceased functioning. Game wardens were still either appointed at the county level or were elected, which caused great inconsistency in enforcement actions. The same game wardens answered to no authority and were often more loyal to their counties than to the chief game warden. There were too few statewide fish and game regulations and too many county-level exceptions to the regulations. And cooperative land deals with the federal government were often handled on an ad hoc basis rather than via planning and budget allocation. The Board of Fisheries was criticized for failure to nurture a successful commercial fishing industry. Only the South Carolina Forestry Commission emerged relatively unscathed, largely because of its successful efforts in education and outreach to the public.

Using data from a recent survey where hunting advocacy groups listed a wide range of factors contributing to game declines (e.g., forest destruction, pollution, siltation of streams and overharvest), Larsen made the point that fish and game administration required more integration, coordination and oversight. He recommended forming a new Department of Natural Resources that would house the South Carolina Forestry Commission, office of chief game warden and the Board of Fisheries, as well as geology and agriculture. This new department would be supervised by one commission and advised by another.[114]

Although the state legislature did not completely accept Larsen's recommendations, it did apparently take his report seriously. In 1952, a reorganization act (1952, Plan No. 8) formed a new South Carolina Wildlife Resources Department to include the State Board of Fisheries, the office of the chief game warden and all previous functions. These units were renamed as divisions: Division of Commercial Fisheries and Division of Game. Oversight of the new department was given to a South Carolina Wildlife Resources Commission, comprising seven members, one from each Congressional district and one at-large. Chief Game Warden Richardson became the first director of the Division of Game and would continue to serve in that job until 1958. James W. Webb replaced him and served from 1959 to 1974.

The reorganization in 1952 occurred in parallel with a rewrite summary of fish and game laws (1952, 898) that addressed some of the issues raised by Larsen in 1947, particularly regarding Division of Game interaction with the federal government on land deals. But most importantly, the various actions taken by state government in 1952 solidified the 1919 claim (1919, 174) that all wild birds, wild game and fish were property of the state. This ushered in a period when the new Division of Game focused much attention and resources on the acquisition of lands and facilities for public hunting and fishing, for wildlife propagation and restoration and for the conservation of rare species and cultural resources. Many of these efforts were done in cooperation with counties, other states, the federal government and nongovernment special interest groups.

It was not by coincidence that a major reorganization of fish and game administration in South Carolina occurred at about the same time as passage of the Federal Aid in Sport Fish Restoration Act (1950). This act was eventually funded by a tax on fishing gear, and the money was funneled back to the states for management and restoration of sport fishes, as well as development of facilities improving public access to lakes and rivers.

PLANTATION LEGACIES

A 1907 article in the *Sunday Outlook* (via the *Columbia State*) described a recent visit by then Audubon secretary Professor T. Gilbert Pearson, who had just completed a field survey of the South Carolina coast in search of opportunities for conserving wildlife.[115] He observed many old rice plantations that were abandoned and grown up in "grasses" but still supported good populations of ducks and quail. At the time, land prices were a fraction of what they had been prior to the Civil War, as no good agricultural product equaled the returns from rice and cutting of timber was done for short-term gain. He recommended landowners lease hunting rights to wealthy northern sportsmen instead of selling them the land. There was concern that wholesale transfer of land from resident farmers and planters to wealthy outsiders would lead to more market hunting and fewer hunting opportunities for South Carolina residents. Indeed, Pearson provided observational details of what is now known in coastal South Carolina as the "second northern invasion," a period of time from 1890 to about 1930 when coastal plantations were acquired by wealthy northern businessmen and then converted to private hunt clubs, opulent residences and leisure plantations.[116] This broad shift in landownership prompted the state legislature to require owners of game preserves greater than five thousand acres to pay a special license tax (1920, 554).

337882   H - Trees, South Carolina, Francis Marion National Forest
Hampton Plantation house. Property of the writer Archibald Rutledge near the Santee River north of F. S. Road No. 42. The live oak in front of the house was saved at the request of George Washington when a guest there.
Taken by Wm. R. Barbour - October 12, 1936.

U. S. DEPARTMENT OF AGRICULTURE
FOREST SERVICE

Opposite, top: Abandoned Hampton Plantation house on the Santee River in 1936. *Courtesy National Archives, identifier number 7003971.*

Opposite, bottom: Restored Hampton Plantation house and grounds in 2020 at the Hampton Plantation State Historic site. *Photo by the author.*

Above: François Flameng's depiction of Napoleon and associates hunting a stag with hounds in a forest at Fontainebleu, circa 1809. European hunting rituals were influential among South Carolina plantation owners. *Courtesy Library of Congress.*

Much has already been written about the transfer of coastal South Carolina plantation land to wealthy northerners. These treatments considered the hidden but sometimes overt desire on the part of wealthy businessmen and their guests to perpetuate antebellum plantation culture;[117] the involvement of African Americans as hunting guides, drivers and laborers;[118] the impact of private and elite hunt clubs on emerging fish and game law;[119] and the hunting practices, particularly baiting and live decoying ducks to impoundments formerly used for commercial rice production.[120] However, less has been written about the fates of plantation land after 1940, when plantation purchases by northerners stopped and a new trend emerged for transfer of these lands to either the public domain or to private residential and commercial development.[121]

Deer hunting party at Hobcaw Barony, circa 1907. *Courtesy the Belle W. Baruch Foundation, Hobcaw Barony.*

African Americans participated in sport hunting of ducks in the early 1900s, often serving as guides, as shown here in Georgetown. *Courtesy Georgetown County Library.*

Two of the first national wildlife refuges designated in coastal South Carolina (see the seventh chapter), Cape Romain and Savannah, reflected the legacy of South Carolina plantations in that historical rice impoundments were included in these refuges. A third refuge added in 1941 was located on the shores of the newly created Santee Cooper lakes, and although not at the coast, it also eventually included impoundments and was ecologically connected to existing coastal refuges. Pinckney Island National Wildlife Refuge, added in 1975, was once part of a plantation and then a private game preserve before it was donated to the U.S. Fish and Wildlife Service. And the Ernest F. Hollings ACE Basin National Wildlife Refuge, added as a refuge in 1990, is mostly former plantation land, including a historical mansion, forests, upland fields and extensive impoundments managed for waterfowl and wading birds. The final refuge added to the coastal South Carolina system in 1997 was the Waccamaw National Wildlife Refuge. It includes large areas of former rice field impoundments and, when taken together with Cape Romain, Ernest F. Hollings and Santee, forms what is known as the Lowcountry Refuge Complex of nearly 115,000 acres. The unique mission of the national wildlife refuge system that primarily focuses

The results of a duck hunt at Hobcaw Barony near Georgetown, circa 1910. *Courtesy the Belle W. Baruch Foundation, Hobcaw Barony.*

A wooden bateau being used for a duck hunting trip. African Americans provided both labor and knowledge during plantation duck hunts, like this one near Beaufort. *Courtesy Beaufort County Library.*

on conservation, management and restoration of wildlife is one that allows refuge managers to pursue actions benefiting wildlife rather than humans pursing wildlife-related activities. Although hunting, fishing and other activities may be allowed and are in some cases encouraged, these are generally restricted in time, place and extent.

In 1940, Chief Game Warden Richardson signaled a shift in state fish and game strategy by pursuing projects that would provide fishing and hunting opportunities for the public. Although not explicitly stated, he certainly understood that the second northern invasion had ended, thus creating opportunities for the state to either lease or buy land for public hunting areas at a time when hunting and fishing in the state were more popular than ever. There were already state parks and national wildlife refuges, but these were for uses other than hunting. In 1941, South Carolina Game and Fish purchased it first property of about six thousand acres, the former Belmont Plantation on the Savannah River, that would eventually become the James W. Webb Wildlife Center and Game Management Area. The acquisition or lease of game management areas was immensely popular, and these lands, programmatically known as Wildlife Management Areas (WMA), in 1971 were identified as places where hunting by the public was allowed but under area-specific restrictions and often with associated fees. Through the 1970s, many of the largest coastal properties purchased or leased and designated as state Wildlife Management Areas were former plantations or hunt clubs and often included mansions, upland forests formerly used for hunting, crops or timbering and, of course, impoundments previously devoted to growing rice or attracting ducks. Good examples of the trend include the Samworth WMA (1,588 acres), Santee Delta WMA (1,722 acres), Santee Coastal Reserve WMA (24,000 acres), Bonneau Ferry WMA (10,712 acres), Bear Island WMA (12,012 acres) and Donnelley WMA (8,048 acres).

The dominance of wetland impoundments and former plantations within the boundaries of many national wildlife refuges and WMAs at the coast of South Carolina is not easily explained. Currently, impounded and formerly impounded wetlands occupy seventy to ninety thousand acres on the South Carolina coast.[122] Although relatively small in area, these wetlands assume high value when placed in the context of wetland draining and filling that has occurred up and down the eastern coast of the United States. However, impoundments are a special class of wetland because of their origins and history. They were typically carved from tidal swamps, ditched, diked and then farmed, all via enslaved labor. When rice farming was no longer possible, a subsistence version of farming continued, but with the primary goal of attracting ducks. Regardless of the management goal, coastal impoundments were and are not sustainable without continuous inputs of materials and labor. Thus, on the one hand, it is odd that federal and state agencies would take on such high-maintenance lands unless, of course, the return in terms of hunting, habitat and wildlife populations was substantial. Miglarese and Sandifer estimated construction and maintenance costs of a typical coastal South Carolina waterfowl impoundment and concluded that these lands represented a "significant" economic investment. There was another liability that emerged when repairs and reimpoundment were attempted. Because the state owns tidal lands, it is required to manage them in the public interest. Some wetland regulators established the position that the best management of coastal impoundments was no management so that over time, as dikes breached and ditches filled, the original wetland ecosystem could emerge. Others held to the idea that the best use was as originally intended: constant management of soils and water levels to encourage certain plant species and discourage other plant species. The controversy of "best use" of coastal impoundments eventually involved private landowners (some impoundments are still privately owned), conservation groups and state and federal agencies, as well as lawyers.

New dike and trunk under construction that will create a brackish marsh impoundment for wading birds. Located on the Tibwin Tract in the Francis Marion National Forest. *Photo by the author.*

New dike with salt marsh on the left and the future impounded brackish marsh on the right. Located on the Tibwin Tract in the Francis Marion National Forest. *Photo by the author.*

Tidal salt marsh and the creek that will provide water on a rising tide to a new impoundment. Located on the Tibwin Tract in the Francis Marion National Forest. *Photo by the author.*

Mud flat that will be flooded to provide shallow brackish water for wildlife, particularly waterfowl and wading birds. Located on the Tibwin Tract in the Francis Marion National Forest. *Photo by the author.*

The search for answers regarding best use of coastal impoundments has involved several working groups, interest groups and individual researchers (e.g., Devoe and Baughman; Folk; and Tufford) all producing lengthy reports. While it is clear that impoundments vary depending on location and river system, the degree of water exchange between the river and the impoundment establishes habitat value for fishes, and the ability to manipulate water levels establishes the habitat value for waterfowl and wading birds. In short, the management choice hinges on the target species. But this is not the entire story:

> *The human perspective about which we are certain is that coastal wetland impoundments have an important place in both the cultural history and current economy of South Carolina. This means that policy decisions will be about much more than just ecology.*[123]

HERITAGE PRESERVES

Started in 1976, the South Carolina Heritage Trust Program was developed to acquire lands for protection of rare species, ecological communities and elements of the state's cultural heritage. In some cases, heritage preserves are relatively small and focus on human-made structures. For example, Daws Island Heritage Preserve is about 1,900 acres and includes four shell rings and other sites of archaeological significance. In contrast, Lewis Ocean Bay Heritage Preserve comprises about 10,000 acres and includes intact Carolina Bays and some of the last remaining populations of the rare Venus flytrap in South Carolina. In recent years, public pressure called for more hunting opportunities on heritage preserves. In response, some of the heritage preserves (e.g., Lewis Ocean Bay) have dual designations as heritage preserve and as WMA. Historic plantations also figure in the elements of some coastal heritage preserves: Botany Bay, Capers Island and Dugannon Plantation. About 38,000 acres of land are included in heritage preserves of coastal South Carolina.

OTHER COASTAL LANDS IN THE PUBLIC INTEREST

Public recognition that coastal South Carolina is a region of relatively high natural capital extends back to the early 1900s, when the Audubon Society mounted its campaign to stop market hunting of birds. These early efforts in monitoring birds and identifying areas important for bird breeding and nesting were critical for helping state and federal agencies prioritize lands for refuge acquisition, including many of the current coastal bird sanctuaries (see TABLE 1). Although South Carolina Audubon owns two sanctuaries in the state, its primary activities at the coast are in identifying important bird areas, educating the public and then developing partnerships for bird conservation. Three of its six current focus areas for habit conservation are located mostly at the coast, again reflecting the continuing importance of this area in conservation.

Other nonprofit entities such as land trusts and the Nature Conservancy are active at the coast. They either take ownership of land for conservation or accept donations of conservation easements. Conservation easements represent a unique method of achieving conservation goals when a private landowner gives up specific land rights in return for a tax deduction. Such easements are done in recognition that deed restrictions on certain land uses contribute to the public interest. As numerous lines of evidence indicate that coastal South Carolina supports relatively high natural capital,[124] nonprofit and public entities focus more of their resources on private lands and processes that encourage private landowners to pursue conservation. Such a trend has roots in South Carolina extending back to 1926, when the chief game warden was instructed to develop game sanctuaries in cooperation with private landowners.

Chapter 9

Fish and Game in the Natural Resources Arena

The Natural Resource Imperative

The environmental movement of the late 1960s and 1970s spawned numerous state and federal changes that continue to shape the fish, game and wildlife landscape of coastal South Carolina. Prior to this time, much of wildlife management focused on game species and managing game populations. But with the public influences of Aldo Leopold's *A Sand County Almanac* and Rachel Carson's *Silent Spring*, there was a recognition that all species were connected to the health of the broader ecosystem and that human actions in these ecosystems could have local and far-reaching impacts. Granted, this was not a novel idea, as early sport hunters in coastal South Carolina wrote about the effects of livestock and fire on game populations (see Chapter 4). The difference emerging in the 1970s was the perspective that *all* species were valid and valuable parts of the ecosystem. Landmark federal environmental legislation such as the Clean Water Act (1972), the Coastal Zone Management Act (1972), the Endangered Species Act (1973) and the Fishery Conservation and Management Act (1976) all reflected the ecosystems approach to managing not just species but the more general class of natural resources. Prior to 1970, the State of South Carolina simply declared all wildlife as property of the state to bolster enforcement of wildlife law. However, in 1971, the path of a conservation movement started in the early 1900s by the Audubon Society came full circle when a state constitutional amendment added "conservation of natural resources" as a matter of public concern.

Soon after passage of the federal Coastal Zone Management Act in 1972, South Carolina passed its parallel version of the law in 1977, the Coastal Tidelands and Wetlands Act. While clearly focused on protecting natural resources of the coast, the Department of Health and Environmental Control (DHEC), formed in 1973 from the Pollution Control Authority and the State Board of Health, was assigned to administer the Coastal Tidelands and Wetlands Act. In addition to regulating environmental impacts and public health, DHEC also oversees the management, harvest and shipping of shellfish, a separate mandate that can be traced back to the Board of Fisheries in 1906.

Although not immediately in tune with the trend to address natural resources broadly rather than in smaller subsets, the State of South Carolina did eventually reorganize its various natural resource administrative units in 1993, a move incorporating many aspects of Larsen's 1947 blueprint. The South Carolina Department of Natural Resources was formed with the following five divisions: Natural Resources Enforcement, Wildlife and Freshwater Fisheries, Marine Resources, Water Resources and Land Resources and Conservation Districts. Several other committees and commissions dealing with wildlife were rolled into the new department, including the state geologist. However, some parts of Larsen's suggestions were ignored: the Commission of Forestry and the Department of Agriculture remained as separate administrative units, a structure that continues to the present.

There is obvious progressive evolution in the State of South Carolina's efforts to manage natural resources in the public interest. Fish and game management started with a small warden force and then progressed to a large warden force and then to an administrative unit where law enforcement is a part of the much larger fish and game management equation, one that includes biologists, ecologists, data scientists, managers of geographic information systems and grant managers. However, some of the same issues noted by Larsen persist, as the entire spectrum of issues affecting natural resources are not administratively integrated. For example, about 80 percent of South Carolina is private forest lands and farms. Land use decisions here are primarily focused on maximizing commodity production, with some efforts to reduce environmental impacts such as nutrient loss to streams. Management of fish, game and wildlife on private forest and cropland is not a priority action because it crosses three different philosophical and administrative realms. Likewise, state parks in South Carolina, originally placed under the Commission of Forestry, were moved to an independent Department of Parks, Recreation and Tourism in 1967. The goal here was to increase recreation and tourism, even though most of the state parks in coastal South Carolina now include exceptional wildlife habitat. Granted, managing natural resources in the public interest is a challenge, particularly when public interests intersect with private interests. Many of the previous points regarding separate administrative structures may be moot if there is good communication and cooperation among state and federal agencies.

Within the Department of Natural Resources, there are also historical influences shaping perceived missions and goals. Fish, game and wildlife were and are the motivations for state acquisition of Wildlife Management Areas and cooperation with the federal government in managing national wildlife refuges. And even with the broader goal of natural resource conservation, there is a focus on public lands located in refuges, preserves and natural areas. However, as Angermeier argues, sound biological conservation in the future must consider processes operating in both natural areas and working lands. Because designated natural areas will never be large enough to incorporate the full range of ecological dynamics and biological diversity, and because development continues to shrink areas of natural habitat, we must identify, appreciate and preserve elements of naturalness in working landscapes as well as nonworking landscapes. ("Naturalness" encompasses historical, current and future ability to support ecological integrity at multiple spatial scales.) By doing this, we may then be able to connect more people to nature and sustain more natural elements over time. As the scientific view of what should be conserved shifts to include working landscapes, so also should the view of conservation value. A few large conservation efforts, including public and private lands, currently exist at the coast of South Carolina. These were developed in response to rapid population growth and urban development at the coast.

ACE BASIN PROJECT

The ACE Basin is a name applied to a large coastal South Carolina region (350,000 acres) drained and fed by three rivers: the Ashepoo, the Combahee and the Edisto. The ACE Basin Task Force, formed in 1988 by a group of public and private entities, established a framework for

Managed impoundments on the ACE Basin National Estuarine Research Reserve. *Courtesy National Oceanic and Atmospheric Administration.*

cooperation to facilitate wise management of natural resources on public wildlife refuges, preserves and private lands. Much of the work of the task force involves educating the public about natural resources of the area in two interpretive centers, providing land management assistance to private landowners, providing hunting opportunities and developing conservation easements. However, direct management of wildlife habitat and monitoring of critical species occurs in several types of refuges: the ACE Basin National Wildlife Refuge, Dugannon Heritage Preserve, the Donnelley Wildlife Management Area, Bear Island Wildlife Management Area, a designated National Estuarine Research Reserve and the Great Swamp Sanctuary. The cooperative effort of the ACE Basin Task Force shows how the knitting together of both public and private conservation lands can produce a landscape likely large enough to support the full range of biological diversity characteristic of the region while at the same time maintaining traditional land uses such as hunting, fishing, forestry and agriculture.

South Carolina Coastal Program

The South Carolina Coastal Program is an effort by the U.S. Fish and Wildlife Service to develop partnerships among private landowners, nongovernment organizations and state agencies to improve habitat for threatened, endangered or at-risk species. The program takes an ecosystem-level approach to conservation, with focus areas located on the coast and farther inland along rivers of the coastal plain. Target habitats include wetlands, uplands, estuaries and beaches. It uses cooperative agreements and grants to facilitate habitat restoration and enhancement for focal species facing threats from development, forestry and climate change. It also facilitates conservation easements on private lands.

Challenges at the Coast

The landscape and natural resources of coastal South Carolina have been manipulated, managed and exploited by various humans beginning with Native Americans and then by a succession of immigrant groups, each one placing unique pressures on the fish, game and wildlife of the region. Beginning in the 1940s after World War II, a novel wave of humans began rolling into coastal South Carolina. One section of that wave comprised seasonal tourists coming to enjoy the beaches and other recreational amenities of the coast. The second section comprised people permanently moving to the coast because of the relatively mild subtropical climate and abundant recreational opportunities provided by the ocean and inshore waterways.

Population pressures have not been evenly distributed along the coast, with Horry and Charleston Counties emerging as a major coastal population centers. Horry County and the Grand Strand, including Myrtle Beach, receive about 15 million tourists per year, but in the last twenty years, the resident population swelled. It is now one of fastest-growing areas in the country. The current Horry County population of about 370,000 people will likely grow to about 517,000 by 2030. Charleston County, including the historic city of Charleston, is also a popular tourist destination but has continued its development as a major coastal economic center, a trend that began nearly three hundred years ago. Outlying municipalities in Berkeley and Dorchester Counties have seen strong residential growth associated with economic development. The population of Charleston County, currently about 420,000, will likely grow to 480,000 by 2030. Although relatively small in terms of population, Beaufort County and Hilton Head have also experienced strong population growth. At present, 27 percent of South Carolina residents live in coastal areas. The increasing human population at the coast of South Carolina is linked to a larger emigration of people from specific midwestern and northern states.

Although trajectories of population growth differ along the South Carolina coast, the important point is the ubiquitous nature of growth. In every situation, development started along the coast and then moved inland. Unlike major coastal urban centers in northern states, where coastal wetlands were historically filled followed by development and then redevelopment, the abundance of forested and agricultural land in South Carolina presented a blank tablet for sketching and then forming a new type of landscape. As such, data from the National Oceanic and Atmospheric Administration (NOAA) shows that from 1996 to 2010, Horry County experienced a 59 percent net increase in developed land, a 22 percent net decrease in forest and a 5 percent net decrease in wetlands. A similar but somewhat muted trend was observed for Charleston County: 18 percent net increase in developed land, 12 percent net decrease in forest and 2 percent net decrease in wetlands. Research attempting to fine-tune these measurements gave similar conclusions. In Horry County, forested wetlands from 1994 to 2006 decreased by 6 percent due to residential development and timber removal.[125] From 1973 to 1991, Charleston County (Mount Pleasant area) had a 30 percent decrease in wetland area and a much larger decrease in forest due to residential development.[126] These trends reveal failures in the prevailing regulatory environment that likely have negative local and downstream impacts on environmental quality, fish, game and wildlife.

The ability of the State of South Carolina to conserve wildlife in the face of changing population pressures should be articulated in the state's comprehensive state wildlife action plan (SWAP). As with many efforts in the history of South Carolina fish and game, the SWAP was stimulated by federal action. Specifically, the State Wildlife Grants Program of 2002 provided funds to the states for wildlife conservation, but in return, a wildlife action plan was required. South Carolina produced its first SWAP in 2005, with modifications in 2010 and 2015. The South Carolina SWAP of 2015 acknowledged that the coastal landscape was changing due to population growth and conversion of forest and agricultural land to residential and commercial uses. And there were also concerns about current and historical loss rates of terrestrial vertebrates and plants. The bulk of the report provided a prioritized list of species of greatest conservation need, with some treatment of game species. Challenges to conservation were provided for each species or group of species. The part of the report focused on the South Carolina Coastal Zone concluded that about 30 percent of the area is currently under some type of conservation protection. However, concurrent population pressures are increasing point and non-point pollution, levels of fisheries harvest and human disturbance of wildlife during critical life history stages. The plan called for more monitoring, better conservation strategies, increased funding for planning (particularly for climate change) and more public/private relationships for large conservation efforts.

Many of the strategies described in the SWAP of 2015 could lay the groundwork for a comprehensive approach to wildlife conservation that includes public and private lands. However, such a planning effort would require participation by state agencies involved in the management of all natural resources, including forests, farmland, air and water. Such a planning effort may perhaps be on a future agenda. Until that time, we can take some comfort in the fact that the rich legacy of coastal fish and wildlife was managed well and will likely be available for enjoyment by future generations.

Chronology of Annotated First Acts

1663. Charter of Carolina, page 2,743. *The Federal and State Constitutions Colonial Charters, and Other Organic Law of the States, Territories and Colonies Now or Heretofore Forming the United States of America*. Compiled and edited by F.N. Thorpe. Washington Government Printing Office, 1909. (Charles II grants the new Province of Carolina to eight of his trusted friends, the lord proprietors.) https://babel.hathitrust.org.

1712. No. 314. An Act for the Better Ordering and Governing of Negroes and Slaves, pages 353–54. *The Statutes at Large of South Carolina: Seventh Volume Containing the Acts Relating to Charleston, Courts, Slaves and Rivers*. Edited by D.J. McCord. Columbia, SC, 1840. (Establishes conditions when slaves can carry guns.) https://www.google.com/books.

1726. No. 519. An Act to Preserve the Navigation and Fishery in the Several Rivers and Creeks in the Province, pages 269–70. *The Statutes at Large of South Carolina: Acts, 1716–1752*, 3rd volume. Edited by T. Cooper. Columbia, SC, 1838. (Regulates obstruction of creeks from cut timber and bans fish poisoning.) https://archive.org/details/statutesatlarge04coopgoog.

1726. No. 521. An Act for the Encouragement of Killing and Destroying Beasts of Prey, page 271. *The Statutes at Large of South Carolina Containing the Acts from 1716, to 1752, Inclusive*, 3rd volume. Edited by T. Cooper. Columbia, SC, 1838. (Offers variable bounties for predators.) https://archive.org/details/statutesatlarge04coopgoog.

1769. No. 988. An Act for the Preservation of Deer, and to Prevent the Mischiefs Arising from Hunting at Unseasonable Times, pages 310–12. *The Statutes at Large of South Carolina: Acts from 1752–1786*, 4th volume. Edited by T. Cooper. Columbia, SC, 1838. (Regulates various aspects of deer hunting including night hunting with fire, trespass, seasons, and purpose.) https://archive.org/details/statutesatlarge05coopgoog.

1789. No. 1463. An Ordinance for the Preservation of Deer; to Prevent the Mischiefs Arising from Fire Hunting and Setting Fire to the Woods, pages 124–26. *The Statutes at Large of South Carolina: Acts, 1786–1814*, 5th volume. Edited by T. Cooper. Columbia, SC, 1839. (Gives local militia the power to enforce game laws.) https://archive.org.

1819. No. 2220. VI. An Act to Provide for the More Effectual Performance of Patrol Duty, page 539. *The Statutes at Large of South Carolina*, 8th volume. Edited by D.J. McCord. Columbia, SC, 1840. (Further clarifies when slaves can carry guns.) https://www.google.com/book.

1847. No. 3024. An Act to Punish and Prevent the Stealing of Oysters, pages 448–49. *Acts of the General Assembly of the State of South Carolina passed in December, 1847*. Columbia, SC, 1848. (Oyster beds protected as private property of citizens.) https://play.google.com/store/books.

1855. No. 4228. An Act to Prohibit Non-Residents from Hunting, Ducking and Fishing within the Limits of This State, page 355. *The Statutes at large of South Carolina*, vol. 12, *Acts from December 1850 to January 1861*. Republican Printing Company, Columbia SC, 1874. (Nonresidents banned from hunting and fishing in South Carolina with some exceptions.) http://www.archive.org.

1865. XIII. An Act to Amend the Criminal Law, page 14. *Reports and Resolutions of the General Assembly of the State of South Carolina, Annual Session of 1865*. Columbia, SC, 1865. (Persons of color not part of the militia but can possess guns used in hunting.) https://books.google.com/books.

1870. No. 4. Joint Resolution Authorizing the Appointment of Fish Commissioners, and Defining the Duties Thereof, pages 416–17. *Acts and Joint Resolutions of the General Assembly of the State of South Carolina Passed at the Regular Session of 1869–70*. Columbia, SC, 1870. (Establishes fish commissioners to enforce fishing regulations.) https://play.google.com.

1870. No. 235. An Act for the Better Protection of Migratory Fish, page 338. *Acts and Joint Resolutions of the General Assembly of the State of South Carolina Passed at the Regular Session of 1869–70.* Columbia, SC, 1870. (Regulates the span of nets across streams and times of fish netting.) https://play.google.com/books.

1871. No. 397. An Act to Amend an Act Entitled "An Act for the Better Protection of Migratory Fish," pages 660–61. *Acts and Joint Resolutions of the General Assembly of the State of South Carolina Passed at the Regular Session of 1870–71.* Columbia, SC, 1871. (Further regulates spans of nets across rivers and obstruction by dams.) https://play.google.com/books.

1872. No. 121. An Act for the Protection and Preservation of Useful Animals, pages 160–61. *Acts and Joint Resolutions of the General Assembly of the State of South Carolina Passed at the Regular Session of 1871–72.* Columbia, SC, 1872. (Sets hunting seasons for game birds and protects insectivorous birds.) https://archive.org/details.

1878. No. 373. An Act to Prevent Fishing with Nets in the Fresh Water Streams of This State at Certain Seasons of the Year, pages 392–93. *Acts and Joint Resolutions of the General Assembly of the State of South Carolina Passed at the Regular Session of 1877–78.* Columbia, SC, 1878. (Sets off-seasons for catching fish in certain counties.) https://play.google.com/books.

1878. No. 600. An Act to Appoint a Fish Commissioner and Increase the Propagation of Fishes, pages 722–23. *Acts and Joint Resolutions of the General Assembly of South Carolina Passed at the Regular Session of 1878*, 16th volume. Columbia, SC, 1878. (Establishes the position of a fish commissioner to propagate fish.) https://archive.org.

1879. No. 104, Section 14. An Act to Create a Department of Agriculture, page 74. *Joint Resolutions of the General Assembly of the State of South Carolina passed at the Regular Session of 1879 and Extra Session of 1880.* Columbia, SC. (Fish commissioner of the state appoints two or more fish wardens in every county.) https://archive.org.

1881. No 472. An Act to Provide a General Stock Law and Regulate the Operations of the Same, pages 591–94. *Acts and Joint Resolutions of the General Assembly of South Carolina Passed at the Regular Session of 1881–1882.* Columbia, SC, 1882. (Requires livestock owners to build fences.)

1884. No. 450. An Act to Prohibit Non-Residents from Hunting, Ducking, Fishing, and Gathering Oysters and Terrapins within the Limits of the Counties of Georgetown, Charleston, Beaufort, Colleton, and Berkeley, Except Upon Certain Conditions, pages 734–35. *Acts and Joint Resolutions of the General Assembly of South Carolina Passed at the Regular Session of 1884.* Columbia, SC, 1885. (Nonresident market hunters and fishermen required to purchase a license.) https://archive.org.

1891. No. 700. An Act to Protect and Encourage the Planting and Cultivation of Shell-Fish within the Waters of This State; for the Appointment of a Fish Commissioner to Authorize the Granting of Franchises for the Use of Certain Land Under Water Belonging to This State and to Make Appropriation Therefor, pages 1,097–1,100. *Acts and Joint Resolutions of the General Assembly of South Carolina Passed at the Regular Session of 1891.* Columbia, SC, 1892. (State oyster beds are leased and regulated.) https://books.google.com/books.

1891. No. 721. An Act to Amend an Act Entitled "An Act to Amend Section 1669 of the General Statutes of the State, in Relation to Fish," Approved December 23, 1889, by Adding a Section Thereto, to Be Designated as Section 3, Providing for a Special Patrol, pages 1,118–20. *Acts and Joint Resolutions of the General Assembly of South Carolina Passed at the Regular Session of 1891.* Columbia, SC, 1892. (Special boat patrol of Waccamaw River to stop illegal netting.) https://books.google.com/books.

1896. No. 101. An Act to Amend Section 1633 General Statutes, Being Section 387 of Revised Statutes, so as to Include Hunting, Shooting and Fishing, pages 220–21. *Acts and Joint Resolutions of the General Assembly of South Carolina Passed at the Regular Session of 1896.* Columbia, SC, 1896. (No hunting or fishing allowed on Sunday.) https://books.google.com/books.

1896. No. 102. An Act to Further Regulate the Catching of Sturgeon and Shad in the Waters of the State, pages 221–22. *Acts and Joint Resolutions of the General Assembly of South Carolina Passed at the Regular Session of 1896.* Columbia, SC, 1896. (Restricts season and methods for taking sturgeon and shad.) https://books.google.com/books.

1896. No. 103. An Act to Prohibit the Catching and Gathering Oysters and Terrapins within the Limits of the State Except Upon Certain Conditions, pages 222–23. *Acts and Joint Resolutions of the General Assembly of South Carolina*

Passed at the Regular Session of 1896. Columbia, SC. (Those gathering oysters and terrapins for sale or export must purchase a license.)

1900. Chapter 552. An Act to Enlarge the Powers of the Department of Agriculture, Prohibit the Transportation by Interstate Commerce of Game Killed in Violation of Local Laws, and for Other Purposes, pages 187–89. *Statutes at Large, 56th Congress.* (The Lacy Act bans interstate traffic in illegally acquired wildlife.) https://www.loc.gov/law.

1905. No. 474. An Act for the Protection of Birds and Their Nests and Eggs, and to Provide for the Punishment of Violations Thereof, pages 950–52. *Acts and Joint Resolutions of the General Assembly of the State of South Carolina Passed at the Regular Session of 1905*, 24th volume. Columbia, SC, 1905. (All wild birds property of the state for the` purpose of regulating market hunting for feathers.) https://babel.hathitrust.org.

1905. No. 489. An Act to Provide for Game Wardens, page 963. *Acts and Joint Resolutions of the General Assembly of the State of South Carolina Passed at the Regular Session of 1905*, 24th volume. Columbia, SC, 1905. (Game wardens established in each county.) https://babel.hathitrust.org.

1906. No. 54. An Act for the Further Protection of Partridges and Quail, page 78. *Acts and Joint Resolutions of the General Assembly of the State of South Carolina Passed at the Regular Session of 1906.* Columbia, SC, 1906. (Regulates the sale of game birds and directs use of fines; nonresidents required to buy license.) https://archive.org/details.

1906. No. 60. An Act to Regulate the Catching, Gathering, Sale, Exporting or Canning of Oysters, Terrapin, Clams, Shad and Sturgeon, to Provide for Licensing Thereof, and to Provide for the Leasing of Public Lands Suitable for the Cultivation Thereof, pages 85–98. *Acts and Joint Resolutions of the General Assembly of the State of South Carolina Passed at the Regular Session of 1906.* Columbia, SC, 1906. (Establishes a Board of Fisheries to regulate catch and sale in the coastal fisheries.) https://archive.org.

1907. No. 315. An Act to Incorporate the Audubon Society of South Carolina, and to Provide for the Preservation of the Wild Birds, Non-Migratory Fish and Animals of the State, pages 659–64. *Acts and Joint Resolutions of the General Assembly of the State of South Carolina Passed at the Regular*

Session of 1907. Columbia, SC, 1907. (South Carolina Audubon formed to enforce game law.) https://babel.hathitrust.org.

1910. No. 291. An Act for the Protection of Game Birds and Animals, and to Provide a Close Season, pages 572–74. *Acts and Joint Resolutions of the General Assembly of the State of South Carolina Passed at the Regular Session of 1910*. Columbia, SC, 1910. (Regulates taking of female deer and sets bag limits on game birds.) https://archive.org.

1910. No. 293. An Act to Provide for a Chief Game Warden, pages 575–76. *Acts and Joint Resolutions of the General Assembly of the State of South Carolina Passed at the Regular Session of 1910*. Columbia, SC, 1910. (Establishes position of chief game warden.) https://books.google.com.

1910. No. 294. An Act for the Protection of Game Fish in the State of South Carolina, and for the Repeal of Certain Laws Relating Thereto, pages 576–78. *Acts and Joint Resolutions of the General Assembly of the State of South Carolina Passed at the Regular Session of 1910*. Columbia, SC, 1910. (Identifies game fish.) https://books.google.com/books.

1915. No. 151. An Act to Provide for a License for Hunters, and a Penalty of Failure to Procure the Same, pages 233–35. *Acts and Joint Resolutions of the General Assembly of the State of South Carolina Passed at the Regular Session of 1915*. Columbia, SC, 1915–16. (Hunting license required for residents.) https://babel.hathitrust.org.

1919. No. 174. An Act to Provide for the Protection of Domestic Birds, Game and Fish, and Provide for a Hunting and Fishing License Therefor, and Provide for the Appointment of Game Wardens. *Acts and Joint Resolutions of the General Assembly of the State of South Carolina Passed at the Regular Session of 1919*. Columbia, SC, 1919. (Fishing license required for nonresidents and certain practices banned.) https://babel.hathitrust.org.

1920. No. 428. An Act to Amend Sections 747 and 748, Criminal Code of 1912, Relating to the Election and Duties of the Chief Game Warden, pages 809–11. *Acts and Joint Resolutions of the General Assembly of the State of South Carolina Passed at the Regular Session of 1920*. Columbia, SC, 1920. (Chief game warden now elected; field wardens appointed.) https://books.google.com/books.

1920. No. 554. An Act Requiring All Persons, Firms, Corporations Holding or Acquiring More than Five Thousand Acres of Land at Any One Time for the Purpose of a Game Preserve for Pleasure to Pay into the Treasuries of the Respective Counties of South Carolina, pages 988–89. *Acts and Joint Resolutions of the General Assembly of the State of South Carolina Passed at the Regular Session of 1920*. Columbia, SC, 1920. (Establishes a tax on large private hunting clubs.) https://babel.hathitrust.org.

1935. (173) No. 113. An Act to Authorize and Empower the State Commission of Forestry to Acquire Property for State Forests and State Parks: to Enter into Cooperative Agreements with the Federal Government and to Pledge Assets in Its Hands for the Retirement of Obligations Incurred in Acquisition of Such Lands, and to Provide for the Use of Revenue from Such Lands. *Acts and Joint Resolutions of the General Assembly of the State of South Carolina Passed at the Regular Session of 1935*. Columbia, SC, 1935. (Gives the Commission of Forestry mandate to establish state parks.) https://babel.hathitrust.org.

1935. (598) No. 336. An Act to Create a Game and Fish Commission, to Provide the Manner of Selecting and Removing the Members Thereof, to Prescribe Its Powers and Duties, and to Make Provision Regarding the Expenses of the Members of Such Commission. *Acts and Joint Resolutions of the General Assembly of the State of South Carolina Passed at the Regular Session of 1935*. Columbia, SC, 1935. (Establishes a Game and Fish Commission.) https://babel.hathitrust.org.

1952. (Plan No. 8) 2890 Statutes at Large, Reorganization Plan No. 8. *Acts and Joint Resolutions of the General Assembly of the State of South Carolina Passed at the Regular Session of 1952*. Columbia, SC, 1952. (Establishes the South Carolina Wildlife Resources Department.) https://babel.hathitrust.org.

1952. No. 898. An Act to Provide for the Propagation, Conservation, and the Hunting of Game and Catching of Fish in This State and to Provide for Punishment for the Violations of the Provisions Thereof, pages 2,179–19. *Acts and Joint Resolutions of the General Assembly of the State of South Carolina Passed at the Regular Session of 1952*. Columbia, SC. (Summary of fish and game regulation to that date with some improvements.) https://babel.hathitrust.org.

1976. Section 49-1-10. Navigable Streams Considered Common Highways; Obstruction as Nuisance. *South Carolina Code of Laws Unannotated*, Title 49—

Waters, Water Resources and Drainage. (Defines navigable waters.) https://www.scstatehouse.gov.

1977. Section 48-39-10 and following. Coastal Tidelands and Wetlands. *South Carolina Code of Laws, Unannotated*, Title 48—Environmental Protection and Conservation. (Establishes protection of coastal resources.) https://www.scstatehouse.gov.

Notes

Chapter 1

1. South Carolina Department of Health and Environmental Control, *Preliminary Analysis of the South Carolina Coastal Zone Boundary*. Using county boundaries to define a political zone is useful, but fish and wildlife do not recognize such boundaries.
2. Strauss, Tebaldi, Kulp, Cutter, Emrich, Rizza and Yawitz, "South Carolina and the Surging Sea." Predicted effects of future climate change are emerging at present.
3. Thorpe, Charter of Carolina, 2,744.
4. Maloney and Ausness, "Use and Legal Significance of the Mean High Water Line," 188.
5. Wyche, "Tidelands and the Public Trust," 143–45. The issue of tideland ownership was vigorously debated in the 1970s. Although never settled, it is not currently a priority focus of wetland regulators.
6. South Carolina's State Wildlife Action Plan (SWAP), South Carolina Department of Natural Resources, October 14, 2014, 5–16.

Chapter 2

7. Roth and Laerm, "Late Pleistocene Vertebrate Assemblage," 1–19. The fossils here were found scattered rather than in strata.

8. National Park Service, "Archaic Shell Rings," 24. The meaning of shell rings is elusive, as many have degraded through time, making interpretation difficult.

9. Ibid., 28.

10. Waddell, *Indians of the South Carolina Lowcountry*, 3–6. Understanding the distribution of Native American tribes in coastal South Carolina is hindered by an almost total absence of reliable maps and data.

11. Stinchcomb, Messner, Driese, Nordt and Stewart, "Pre-Colonial... Sedimentation," 363–66. Such evidence would be lacking in coastal South Carolina, where sedimentation patterns along coastal rivers are obscure.

12. Fowler and Konopik, "History of Fire in the Southern United States," 165. Currently, many ecosystem management efforts attempt to mimic prehistoric fire regimens.

13. Brown, "Wildland Burning by American Indians in Virginia," 29.

14. Holt, "Hunting," 3–7.

15. Waddell, *Indians of the South Carolina Lowcountry*, 38. There is much conjecture here, as records are sparse.

16. Rivers, *Sketch of the History of South Carolina*, 26. The frequent mention of cornfields suggests that Native American agriculture at the coast was extensive.

17. Hilton, "Relation of a Discovery," 44, 45, 53.

18. Ashe, "Carolina, or a Description of the Present State," 150.

19. Wilson, "Account of the Province of Carolina," 170.

20. Edgar, *South Carolina*, 135. The emergence of deerskin as a valuable commodity probably led to much deer harvest and waste of deer meat.

21. Mathews, "Contemporary View of Carolina in 1680," 157. Understanding Native American fishing methods at the coast is hindered by the fact that gear rapidly decayed and was not preserved.

22. Wood, "It Was a Negro Taught Them," 33–44.

23. Goode, *Fisheries and Fishery Industries of the United States*, 510.

24. Wood, *Discovering Afro-America*, 33. The use of fish poisons by American Indians and African Americans is not well studied or understood.

Chapter 3

25. Wood, *Discovering Afro-America*, 34.

26. Weir, *Colonial South Carolina*, 37.

27. Kline, *First Along the River*, 29. The effects of livestock grazing on ecological communities are well studied in western U.S rangeland. Such effects are not well understood in southeast coastal systems.

28. Edgar, *South Carolina*, 139.

29. Ibid.

30. Luken, "What the Land Reveals," 27. Many historical rice fields have never reverted to the original swamp forests, even as the rice field dikes decayed and a relatively normal tidal cycle was restored.

31. Joyner, *Down by the Riverside*, 100. The conclusions reached here were from interviews.

32. Michie, *Richmond Hill Plantation*, 130–32. The conclusions reached here were the result of extensive excavations near slave quarters.

33. Ibid., 133.

34. Ibid., 135.

35. Heyward, *Seed from Madagascar*, 123. Heyward described in detail how one slave used a massive gun to regularly eliminate large quantities of nuisance ducks.

36. Belin, *Sandy Island Plantation Journal*, 30.

Chapter 4

37. Brock and Vivian, introduction, *Leisure, Plantations, and the Making of the New South*, 5.

38. Childs, *Rice Planter and Sportsman*, 82. This publication best captures the abundance of fish and game that once existed at the coast.

39. Elliott, *Carolina Sports by Land and Water*, 283. Elliott was a true sportsman and naturalist at heart and often found himself in conflict with prevailing views.

40. Kline, *First Along the River*, 39.

41. Childs, *Rice Planter and Sportsman*, 58.

42. Elliott, *Carolina Sports by Land and Water*, 283–84.

43. Heyward, *Seed from Madagascar*, 117.

44. Elliott, *Carolina Sports by Land and Water*, 292.

45. Ibid., 285.

46. Ibid., 286.

47. Ibid., 292.

Chapter 5

48. Kline, *First Along the River*, 39. In coastal South Carolina, the transition away from a farming/natural resource–based economy was and is relatively slow, except in the case of tourism.

49. Goode, *Fisheries and Fishery Industries of the United States*, xvi.

50. U.S. Commission of Fish and Fisheries, *Report of the Commissioner for 1882*, part 10, 947. These carp would eventually spread throughout the country but never became accepted as food.

51. *Sunday Outlook*, "Meeting of County Commissioners." Local counties had to interpret the laws and then found it nearly impossible to enforce the laws due to a lack of wardens.

52. U.S. Commission of Fish and Fisheries, *Report of the Commissioner for 1872 and 1873*, part 2, 397. Population declines of fish were observed in the late 1800s across the eastern United States.

53. Johnson, "Marketing of Shad on the Atlantic Coast," 2.

54. Walburg and Nichols, "Biology and Management of the American Shad," 34.

55. Tighe, "Georgetown as It Will Be."

56. Donaldson, "Fishing Industry."

57. Davis, "Illegal Fishing." Winyah Bay and its associated rivers represented a large area that was almost impossible to monitor for illegal fishing activity. The situation persists to the present; *Kingstree County Record*, "Scarcity of Shad."

58. *News and Courier*, "Fish Culture in South Carolina."

59. Walburg and Nichols, "Biology and Management of the American Shad," 34.

60. Michie, *Richmond Hill Plantation*, 130.

61. Donaldson, "Fishing Industry."

62. Goode, *Fisheries and Fishery Industries of the United States*, 502.

63. Morgan, "Notice."

64. Folk, "On the Salt Sea." The harvest of very large fish, as occurred in the late 1800s and early 1900s, essentially eliminated the spawning base and thus set the stage for fish population declines. Current regulations protect spawning individuals via size limits.

65. Elliot, *Carolina Sports*, 124.

66. Goode, *Fisheries and Fishery Industries of the United States*, 512.

67. Coker, "Cultivation of the Diamond-Back Terrapin," 49. The culture of terrapin was not a successful enterprise.

68. Goode, *Fisheries and Fishery Industries of the United States*, 503.

69. Ibid.

70. Coker, "Cultivation of the Diamond-Back Terrapin," 14.

71. *Georgetown Times*, "Wouldst Breed Terrapin."

72. Goode, *Fisheries and Fishery Industries of the United States*, 506.

73. Ibid.

74. Ibid., 507.

75. Ibid., 510.

76. Wood, *Discovering Afro-America*, 33.

77. Burrell, "Oyster Industry of South Carolina," 26. The oyster industry in coastal South Carolina was the focus of numerous investigations of child labor practices. Problems of pollution in the oyster beds persist to the present.

78. Daniel, "Plume Hunters," 19.

79. Cart, "Lacey Act," 4. The Lacey Act was a landmark legislation, but enforcement was weak due to lack of personnel.

80. Dunlap, "Sport Hunting and Conservation," 53.

81. *Forest and Stream*, "Palmetto Gun Club." This action reflects the perception that enforcement of fish and game laws was lax.

Chapter 6

82. Pearson, "South Carolina Game Law," 697. Putting enforcement of fish and game law into the hands of the Audubon Society suggests that state legislators were seeking an easy fix to the problem. Or perhaps they did not want to see the problem fixed.

83. Rice, "State Audubon Reports," *Bird Lore* 12 (1910): 302.

84. *Georgetown Daily Item*, "Vanishing of the Shad."

85. *Forest and Stream*, "Sportsmen and Shooting Fees," 256.

86. Rice, "State Audubon Reports," *Bird Lore* 13 (1911): 382. This passage well characterizes the strong resistance of state legislators to fish and game protections.

87. Blease, "Message from the Governor," 541.

88. *Herald and News*, "Feudal Disregard of Lawmaking Body."

89. Pearson, "Aigrette Traffic," 277–78.

90. Rice, "Report of James Henry Rice Jr.," 399. Rice was an underappreciated figure of conservation in coastal South Carolina. He was singularly focused on bird preservation and did much to change the existing regulatory landscape. He had a hard time in Columbia.

91. Forbush, "Strange that Our Game Is Gone," 695.

Chapter 7

92. *Forest and Stream*, "Sportsmen and Shooting Fees," 256.

93. Richardson, Report of A.A. Richardson, Season 1922–1923, 4; Fiscal Year July 1, 1923–June 30, 1924, 5. In his reports, Richardson always let legislators know that his warden enterprise was self-sustaining, efficient and a contributor to the public good.

94. Richardson, Report of A.A. Richardson, Fiscal Year, July 1, 1927–June 30, 1928, 4.

95. Ibid., Fiscal Year, July 1, 1929–June 30, 1930, 4.

96. Ibid., Fiscal Year, July 1, 1932–June 30, 1933, 4. This authorization set the stage for future acquisition of a much larger system of Wildlife Management Areas and wildlife refuges.

97. Ibid., 5.

98. Ibid., Fiscal Year, July 1, 1939–June 30, 1940, 5. Cooperation between the State of South Carolina and the federal government was facilitated by a steady flow of resources from Washington, D.C.

99. Lee, "Pragmatic Migratory Bird Treaty Act," 652. Review of this legislation reveals the difficulties of protecting natural resources that are mobile and may travel across state and country boundaries.

100. Migratory Bird Conservation Commission, *Review of the Work for 1930*, 4. It is informative to compare and contrast the political landscape in the 1930s that allowed rapid development of a refuge system with the current landscape.

101. Richardson, Report of A.A. Richardson, Fiscal Year, July 1, 1936–June 30, 1937, 3.

102. Ibid., 4.

103. Ibid., Fiscal Year, July 1, 1939–June 30, 1940, 4. It is ironic that the federal government provided funds to build fish hatcheries, while the State of South Carolina lagged in providing personnel to run the hatcheries.

104. Ibid., 5.

105. Bradley, Kjerfve and Morris, "Rediversion Salinity Change in the Cooper River," 374. The effects of diversion spread well beyond water to adjacent wetlands.

106. Richardson, Report of A.A. Richardson, Fiscal Year, July 1, 1940–June 30, 1941, 7. Opposition to the lake project was likely strong among those who would lose their land.

107. Parkman, "History of the Waterways," 24.

108. U.S. Army Corps of Engineers, "Dredged Material Management Plan," 29.

109. Smith, *State of South Carolina Report...July 1 1934 to June 30, 1935*, 31. South Carolina state parks were originally identified for recreation, but over time they have assumed some traits of wildlife refuges and nature preserves. Hunting is still not allowed.

110. Hester, "Establishing the Francis Marion," 59.

111. Ibid., 61.

112. Richardson and Kirchner, "United States Department of Agriculture," 296–98. The details of this agreement show the complicated negotiations involved when a large area of land is placed in the public domain.

Chapter 8

113. Larsen, *South Carolina's Natural Resources*, 195–97. We do not know the impetus for Larsen's report. However, he was straightforward in documenting the successes and failures of state government to manage natural resources.

114. Ibid., 198.

115. *Columbia State*, "Our Game Preserves." Pearson would likely be very surprised to see how many of the historical rice plantations in coastal South Carolina have been converted to housing developments.

116. Lockhart, "Rice Planters in Their Own Right," 107.

117. Vivian, "Plantation Life," 27.

118. Smith, "Knowledge of the Hunt," 133.

119. Lee, "Pragmatic Migratory Bird Treaty Act," 679.

120. Miglarese and Sandifer, "Ecological Characterization of South Carolina Wetland Impoundments," 95. Maintenance of coastal impoundments includes the following: regular clearing of trunks, trunk repair, dike repair and reinforcement, frequent inspection and vegetation management.

121. Kovacik, "South Carolina Rice Coast Landscape Changes," 55–61. This type of assessment would now require the inclusion of residential development as a driver of landscape change.

122. Tompkins, "Scope and Status of Coastal Wetland Impoundments," 35.

123. Tufford, "State of Knowledge Report," 43. After compiling much scientific data, Tufford concluded that human history and culture are just as important as scientific data in determining land management goals.

124. Luken, "Abandoning Risky Agriculture and Leveraging Natural Capital," 48. Due to relatively high natural capital in the form of wildlife refuges, rare species and wetlands, some counties may be better suited for conservation than agriculture.

Chapter 9

125. Swords, "Wetlands Status and Trends for Horry County," 5. This trend in landscape change continues to the present.
126. All and Nelson, "Remote Sensing Quantification," 95.

Sources

All, J., and J. Nelson. "Remote Sensing Quantification of Wetland Habitat Change in South Carolina: Implications for Coastal Resource Policy." *Geographical Bulletin* 50 (2008): 87–101. https://gammathetaupsilon.org.

Angermeier, P.L. "The Natural Imperative for Biological Conservation." *Conservation Biology* 14 (2000): 373–81.

Ashe, T. "Carolina, or a Description of the Present State of that Country, by Thomas Ashe, 1682." In *Narratives of Early Carolina*. Edited by A.S. Salley Jr. New York: Charles Scribner's Sons, 1911.

Belin, A. *Sandy Island Plantation Journal* 2 (1797–98). Lowcountry Digital Library, South Carolina Historical Society.

Blease, C.L. "Message from the Governor." *Journal of the Senate of the General Assembly of the State of South Carolina* (1913). https://play.google.com/books/reader.

Bradley, P.M., B. Kjerfve and J.T. Morris. "Rediversion Salinity Change in the Cooper River, South Carolina: Ecological Implications." *Estuaries* 13 (1990): 373–79.

Braund, K.E. *Deerskins & Duffels: The Creek Indian Trade with Anglo-America, 1685–1815.* Lincoln: University of Nebraska Press, 1993.

Brock, J., and D. Vivian. Introduction to *Leisure, Plantations, and the Making of the New South: The Sporting Plantations of the South Carolina Lowcountry and Red Hills Region, 1900–1940.* Edited by J. Brock and D. Vivian. Lanham, MD: Lexington Books, 2015.

Broughton, J.M., and E.M. Weitzel. "Population Reconstructions for Humans and Megafauna Suggest Mixed Causes for North American Pleistocene Extinctions." *Nature Communications* 9 (2018): 5,441. https://doi.org/10.1038/s41467-018-07897-1.

Brown, H. "Wildland Burning by American Indians in Virginia." *Fire Management Today* 60 (2000): 29–39. https://www.fs.usda.gov.

Burrell, V.G., Jr. "The Oyster Industry of South Carolina." Marine Resources Library, South Carolina Marine Resources Center, 2003. http://mrl.cofc.edu.

Cart, T.W. "The Lacey Act: America's First Nationwide Wildlife Statute." *Forest History Newsletter* 17 (1973): 4–13. DOI: 10.2307/4004266. https://www.jstor.org.

Childs, A.R., ed. *Rice Planter and Sportsman: The Recollections of J. Motte Alston, 1821–1909.* Columbia: University of South Carolina Press, 1999.

Cioc, M. *The Game of Conservation: International Treaties to Protect the World's Migratory Animals.* Athens: Ohio University Press, 2009.

Coker, R.E. "The Cultivation of the Diamond-Back Terrapin." *Bulletin No. 14* (1906). The North Carolina Geological Survey. https://books.google.com/books.

Columbia State. "Our Game Preserves, the Best Duck and Quail Shooting in the Country Right Here. Prof. Pierson Investigates." Reprinted in the *Sunday Outlook*, April 27, 1907. http://www.gcdigital.org.

Cook, S., J. Hudson, N. Meriwether and P. Coclanis. *Twilight on the South Carolina Rice Fields: Letters of the Heyward Family, 1862–1871.* Edited by M. Hollis and A. Stokes. Columbia: University of South Carolina Press, 2010.

Coughlan, M.R., and D.R. Nelson. "Influences of Native American Land Use on the Colonial Euro-American Settlement of the South Carolina Piedmont." *PlosOne* 13, no. 3 (2018). https://doi:10.1371/journal.pone.0195036.

Cronon, W., and R. White. "Indians in the Land." *American Heritage* 37 (1986): 18–25. https://www.americanheritage.com.

Daniel, J. "The Plume Hunters." *North Carolina Wildlife* (May/June 2014): 18–22. https://www.ncwildlife.org.

Davis, D.B. "Illegal Fishing: An Up-Countryman Proposes to Remedy the Evil by Forbidding the Use of Seines, an Absurd Proposition." *Georgetown Enquirer*, March 27, 1889. http://www.gcdigital.org.

Décima, E.B., and D.F. Dincauze. "The Boston Back Bay Fish Weirs." In *Hidden Dimensions: The Cultural Significance of Wetland Archaeology.* Edited by K. Bernick. Vancouver, CAN: UBC Press, 2011.

DeVoe, M.R., and D.S. Baughman, eds. *South Carolina Coastal Wetland Impoundments: Ecological Characterization, Management, Status, and Use*. Vol. 2, *Technical Synthesis*. Publication no. SC-SG-TR-82-2. Charleston, SC: South Carolina Sea Grant Consortium, 1986. https://ecos.fws.gov.

Donaldson, R.J. "The Fishing Industry: A Comprehensive Survey of the Subject." *Georgetown Enquirer*, November 7, 1887. http://www.gcdigital.org.

Dunlap, T.R. "Sport Hunting and Conservation, 1880–1920." *Environmental Review* 12 (1988): 51–60. https://www.jstor.org.

Edgar, W. *South Carolina: A History*. Columbia: University of South Carolina Press, 1998.

Elliott, W. *Carolina Sports by Land and Water Including Incidents of Devil-Fishing, Wild-Cat, Deer and Bear Hunting etc.* New York: Darby and Jackson, 1859.

Ellsworth, D.L., L. Rodney, R.L. Honeycutt, N.J. Silvy, M.H. Smith, J.W. Bickham and W.D. Klimstra. "White-Tailed Deer Restoration to the Southeastern United States: Evaluating Genetic Variation." *Journal of Wildlife Management* 58 (1994): 686–97. https://doi:10.2307/3809683.

Facey, D.E., and H.J. Van Den Avyle. "Species Profiles: Life Histories and Environmental Requirements of Coastal Fishes and Invertebrates (South Atlantic)—American Shad." *U.S. Fish and Wildlife Service Biological Report* 82, 11.45 (1986). U.S. Army Corps of Engineers. TR EL-82-4.

Folk, J.W. "On the Salt Sea." Reprinted in the *Georgetown Enquirer*, June 24, 1885. http://www.gcdigital.org.

Folk, T.H., E.P. Wiggers, D. Harrigal and M. Purcel, eds. *Rice Fields for Wildlife: History, Management Recommendations and Regulatory Guidelines for South Carolina's Managed Tidal Impoundments*. Yemassee, SC: Nemours Wildlife Foundation, 2016. https://www.manomet.org.

Forbush, E.H. "Strange that Our Game Is Gone." *Forest and Stream*, October 29, 1910. https://babel.hathitrust.org.

Forest and Stream. "The Palmetto Gun Club." October 6, 1900. https://babel.hathitrust.org.

———. "Sportsmen and Shooting Fees." February 18, 1911. https://babel.hathitrust.org.

Fowler, C., and E. Konopik. "The History of Fire in the Southern United States." *Human Ecology Review* 14 (2007): 165–76. https://www.humanecologyreview.org.

Georgetown Daily Item. "The Vanishing of the Shad: Ruinous Revenue by the State Depleting the Shad Industry." April 22, 1909. http://www.gcdigital.org.

Georgetown Times. "Wouldst Breed Terrapin." June 11, 1913. http://www.gcdigital.org.

Gibbons, J.W., J.E. Lovich, A.D. Tucker, N.N. Fitzsimmons and J.L. Greene. "Demographic and Ecological Factors Affecting Conservation and Management of the Diamondback Terrapin (*Malaclemys terrapin*) in South Carolina." *Chelonian Conservation and Biology* 4 (2001): 66–74.

Gilbert, C.R. "Species Profiles: Life Histories and Environmental Requirements of Coastal Fishes and Invertebrates (Mid-Atlantic Bight), Atlantic and Shortnose Sturgeons." *U.S. Fish and Wildlife Service Biological Report* 82, 11.122 (1989). U.S. Army Corps of Engineers. TR EL-82-4.

Goode, G.B. *The Fisheries and Fishery Industries of the United States: Section II, Geographical Review of the Fisheries Industries and Fishing Communities for the Year 1880.* U.S. Commission of Fish and Fisheries, Washington, D.C., 1887. https://play.google.com.

Greer, A. "Commons and Enclosure in the Colonization of North America." *American Historical Review* 117 (2012): 365–86. https://doi.org/10.1086/ahr.117.2.365.

Harris, L.B. *Patroons and Periaguas: Enslaved Watermen and Watercraft of the Lowcountry.* Columbia: University of South Carolina Press, 2014.

Herald and News. "Feudal Disregard of Lawmaking Body." March 2, 1917. https://historicnewspapers.sc.edu.

Hester, A. "Establishing the Francis Marion, National Forest History in South Carolina's Lowcountry, 1901–1936." *Forest History Today* (Spring/Fall 2011): 56–63. https://foresthistory.org.

Heyward, D.C. *Seed from Madagascar.* Columbia: University of South Carolina Press, 1993.

Hilton, W. "A Relation of a Discovery, by William Hilton, 1664." In *Narratives of Early Carolina, 1650–1708.* Edited by A.S. Salley Jr. New York: Charles Scribner's Sons, 1911.

Hockensmith, B.L. "Flow and Salinity Characteristics of the Santee River Estuary, South Carolina." *South Carolina Department of Natural Resources Water Resources Report* 35 (2004). https://dc.statelibrary.sc.gov.

Holt, J. "Hunting: A (Native) American Tradition." *Illinois Antiquity* 45 (2010): 3–7.

Irwin, R.S. *The Providers, Hunting and Fishing Methods of the North American Natives.* Blaine, WA: Hancock House Publishers, 1984.

Johnson, F.F. "Marketing of Shad on the Atlantic Coast." U.S. Department of Commerce, Bureau of Fisheries, Washington, D.C., 1938. https://books.google.com/books.

Joyner, C. *Down by the Riverside: A South Carolina Slave Community.* Urbana: University of Illinois Press, 1984.

Kawashima, Y., and R. Tone. "Environmental Policy in Early America: A Survey of Colonial Statutes." *Journal of Forest History* 27 (1983): 168–79. https://doe: 10.2307/4004898.

Kingstree County Record. "Scarcity of Shad." Reprinted in *Georgetown Semi-Weekly Times*, March 11, 1893.

Kline, B. *First Along the River: A Brief History of the U.S. Environmental Movement.* San Francisco, CA: Acada Books, 1997.

Kovacik, C.F. "South Carolina Rice Coast Landscape Changes." *Proceedings of the Tall Timbers Ecology and Management Conference* 16 (1979): 47–65.

Larsen, C. *South Carolina's Natural Resources: A Study in Public Administration.* Columbia: University of South Carolina Press, 1947. https://babel.hathitrust.org.

Lee, H-J L. "The Pragmatic Migratory Bird Treaty Act: Protecting 'Property.'" *Boston College Environmental Affairs Law Review* 31 (2004): 649–81. http://lawdigitalcommons.bc.edu.

Lockhart, M.A. "'Rice Planters in Their Own Right': Northern Sportsmen and Waterfowl Management on the Santee River Plantations during the Baiting Era, 1905–1935." In *Leisure, Plantations, and the Making of the New South: The Sporting Plantations of the South Carolina Lowcountry and Red Hills Region, 1900–1940.* Edited by J. Brock and D. Vivian. Lanham, MD: Lexington Books, 2015.

Luken, J.O. "Abandoning Risky Agriculture and Leveraging Natural Capital: A County-Level Method for Identifying Conservation Opportunity." *Natural Areas Journal* 40 (2020): 45–50. https://doi.org/10.3375/043.040.0106.

———. "What the Land Reveals: A Journey into a Low Country Rice Plantation." *South Carolina Review* 47 (2015): 141–46. https://cup.sites.clemson.edu.

Maloney, F.E., and R.C. Ausness. "The Use and Legal Significance of the Mean High Water Line in Coastal Boundary Mapping." *North Carolina Law Review* 53 (1974): 185–273. http://scholarship.law.unc.edu.

Mathews, M. "A Contemporary View of Carolina in 1680." *South Carolina Historical Magazine* 55 (1954): 153–59. https://www.jstor.org.

McPhee, J. *The Founding Fish.* Farrar, New York: Straus & Giroux, 2002.

Michie, J.L. *Richmond Hill Plantation, 1810–1868: The Discovery of Antebellum Life on a Waccamaw River Plantation.* Spartanburg, SC: Reprint Company, 1990.

Miglarese, J.V., and P.A. Sandifer. "An Ecological Characterization of South Carolina Wetland Impoundments." *Technical Report Number 51* (1982). Marine Resources Research Institute, Charleston, SC. https://mrl.cofc.edu.

Migratory Bird Conservation Commission (MBCC). *Review of the Work for 1930, House of Representatives Document No. 670* (1930). https://ecos.fws.gov.

Morgan, W.D. "Notice." *Georgetown Semi-Weekly Times*, August 24, 1895. http://www.gcdigital.org.

Murphy, E. "The Eighteenth-Century Southeastern American Indian Economy." In *The Other Side of the Frontier, Economic Explorations into Native American History.* Edited by L. Barrington. Boulder, CO: Westview Press, 1999.

National Oceanic and Atmospheric Administration (NOAA). Coastal Change Analysis Program (C-CAP) Regional Land Cover, Landcover Atlas. Charleston, SC: NOAA Office for Coastal Management, 2020. www.coast.noaa.gov/ccapftp.

National Park Service. "Archaic Shell Rings of the Southeast U.S., National Historic Landmarks Historic Context." NPS Form 10-900-a, revised August 2002. OMB No. 1024-0018. http://www.npshistory.com.

News and Courier. "Fish Culture in South Carolina." Reprinted in the *Georgetown Enquirer*, March 18, 1885.

Parkman, A. "History of the Waterways of the Atlantic Coast of the United States." *Navigation History NWS-83-10* (1983). U.S. Army Engineer Water Resources Support Center. https://babel.hathitrust.org.

Paveo-Zuckerman, B. "Creek Subsistence and Economic Strategies in the Historic Period." *American Antiquity* 72 (2007): 5–33.

Pearson, T.G. "Aigrette Traffic." *Bird Lore* 13 (1911): 277–78. https://babel.hathitrust.org.

———. "South Carolina Game Law." *Forest and Stream*, May 4, 1907. https://babel.hathitrust.org.

Rice, J.H., Jr. "Report of James Henry Rice Jr., Field Agent for South Carolina." *Bird Lore* 14 (1912): 398–402. https://babel.hathitrust.org.

———. "State Audubon Reports, South Carolina." *Bird Lore* 13 (1911): 381–82. https://babel.hathitrust.org.

———. "State Audubon Reports, South Carolina." *Bird Lore* 12 (1910): 302–3. https://babel.hathitrust.org.

Richardson, A.A. Report of A.A. Richardson, Chief Game Warden of the State of South Carolina, Fiscal Year, July 1, 1940–June 30, 1941. https://babel.hathitrust.org.

———. Report of A.A. Richardson, Chief Game Warden of the State of South Carolina, Fiscal Year, July 1, 1939–June 30, 1940. https://babel.hathitrust.org.

———. Report of A.A. Richardson, Chief Game Warden of the State of South Carolina, Fiscal Year, July 1, 1936–June 30, 1937. https://babel.hathitrust.org.

———. Report of A.A. Richardson, Chief Game Warden of the State of South Carolina, Fiscal Year, July 1, 1932–June 30, 1933. https://babel.hathitrust.org.

———. Report of A.A. Richardson, Chief Game Warden of the State of South Carolina, Fiscal Year, July 1, 1929–June 30, 1930. https://babel.hathitrust.org.

———. Report of A.A. Richardson, Chief Game Warden of the State of South Carolina, Fiscal Year, July 1, 1927–June 30, 1928. https://babel.hathitrust.org.

———. Report of A.A. Richardson, Chief Game Warden of the State of South Carolina, Fiscal Year, July 1, 1923–June 30, 1924. https://babel.hathitrust.org.

———. Report of A.A. Richardson, Chief Game Warden of the State of South Carolina, Season 1922–1923. https://babel.hathitrust.org.

Richardson, A.A., and J.C. Kirchner. "United States Department of Agriculture, Forest Service—Cooperative Agreement with the Department of Fish and Game, State of South Carolina." 1937. In *Calendar No. 1222, Senate Report No. 1183*, printed in 1940. https://play.google.com/books.

Rivers, W.J. *A Sketch of the History of South Carolina to the Close of the Proprietary Government by the Revolution of 1719*. Charleston, SC: McCarter and Company, 1856.

Roth, J.A., and J. Laerm. "A Late Pleistocene Vertebrate Assemblage from Edisto Island, South Carolina." *Brimleyana* 3 (1980): 1–29. http://digital.ncdcr.gov.

Silver, T. *A New Face on the Countryside, Indians, Colonists, and Slaves in the South Atlantic Forests, 1500–1800*. Cambridge, UK: Cambridge University Press, 1990.

Smith, H.A. *State of South Carolina Report of the State Commission of Forestry for the Year July 1, 1934 to June 30, 1935*. 1935. https://dc.statelibrary.sc.gov.

———. *State of South Carolina Report of the State Commission of Forestry for the Year July 1, 1933 to June 30, 1934*. 1934. https://dc.statelibrary.sc.gov.

Smith, H.R. "Knowledge of the Hunt: African American Guides in the South Carolina Lowcountry at the Turn of the Twentieth Century." In *Leisure, Plantations, and the Making of the New South: The Sporting Plantations of the South Carolina Lowcountry and Red Hills Region, 1900–1940*. Edited by J. Brock and D. Vivian. Lanham, MD: Lexington Books, 2015.

Smith, T.I.J. "The Fishery, Biology, and Management of Atlantic Sturgeon, *Acipenser oxyrhynchus*, in North America." *Environmental Biology of Fishes* 14 (1985): 61–72. https://doi.org/10.1007/BF0000157.

South Carolina Department of Health and Environmental Control (SCDHEC). *Preliminary Analysis of the South Carolina Coastal Zone Boundary*, 2016. https://www.scdhec.gov.

South Carolina Historical Society (SCHS). "Granting of Land in Colonial South Carolina." *South Carolina Historical Magazine* 77 (1976): 208–12. https://www.jstor.org.

South Carolina's State Wildlife Acton Plan (SWAP). South Carolina Department of Natural Resources, Final, October 14, 2014. http://dnr.sc.gov.

Stern, J. *The Lives in Objects: Native Americans, British Colonists, and Cultures of Labor and Exchange in the Southeast.* Chapel Hill: University of North Carolina Press, 2017.

Stinchcomb, G.E., T.C. Messner, S.G. Driese, L.C. Nordt and R.M. Stewart. "Pre-Colonial (A.D. 1100–1600) Sedimentation Related to Prehistoric Maize Agriculture and Climate Change in Eastern North America." *Geology* 39 (2011): 363–66. https://doi.org/10.1130/G31596.1.

Strauss, B., C. Tebaldi, S. Kulp, S. Cutter, C. Emrich, D. Rizza and D. Yawitz. "South Carolina and the Surging Sea: A Vulnerability Assessment with Projections for Sea Level Rise and Coastal Flood Risk." Climate Central Research Report, 2014. https://sealevel.climatecentral.org.

Sunday Outlook. "Meeting of County Commissioners." December 16, 1905. http://www.gcdigital.org.

Swords, J.Q. "Wetlands Status and Trends for Horry County, South Carolina: 1994–2006." U.S. Fish and Wildlife Service, National Wetlands Inventory Program, Southeast Region, Atlanta, Georgia, 2012. https://pdfs.semanticscholar.org.

Tighe, M.F. "Georgetown as It Will Be: A Record of the Revival in the Riverside City, the Shad Fisheries." Reprinted in the *Georgetown Enquirer*, February 22, 1888. http://www.gcdigital.org.

Tompkins, M.W. "Scope and Status of Coastal Wetland Impoundments in South Carolina." In *South Carolina Coastal Wetland Impoundments: Ecological Characterization, Management, Status, and Use.* Vol. 2, *Technical Synthesis. Publication No. SC-SG-TR-82-2.* Edited by M.R. DeVoe and D.S. Baughman. Charleston, SC: South Carolina Sea Grant Consortium, 1986. https://ecos.fws.gov.

Tufford, D.L. "State of Knowledge Report, South Carolina Coastal Wetland Impoundments." South Carolina Sea Grant Consortium, 2005. https://www.scseagrant.org.

U.S. Army Corps of Engineers (USACE). "Dredged Material Management Plan, Atlantic Intracoastal Waterway, Port Royal Sound, South Carolina to Cumberland Sound, Georgia." Savannah District U.S. Army Corps of Engineers, 2015. https://www.sas.usace.army.mil.

U.S. Commission of Fish and Fisheries (USCFF). *Report of the Commissioner for 1882*, part 10. Washington, D.C., 1884. https://books.google.com.

———. *Report of the Commissioner for 1872 and 1873*, part 2. Washington, D.C., 1874. https://babel.hathitrust.org.

———. *Report of the Commissioner for the Year Ending June 30, 1903*, part 29. Washington, D.C., 1905. https://books.google.com.

Vivian, D. "'Plantation Life': Varieties of Experience on the Remade Plantations of the South Carolina Lowcountry." In *Leisure, Plantations, and the Making of the New South: The Sporting Plantations of the South Carolina Lowcountry and Red Hills Region, 1900–1940*. Edited by J. Brock and D. Vivian. Lanham, MD: Lexington Books, 2015.

Waddell, G. *Indians of the South Carolina Lowcountry, 1562–1751*. Spartanburg, SC: Reprint Company, 1980.

Walburg, C.H., and P.R. Nichols. "Biology and Management of the American Shad and Status of the Fisheries, Atlantic Coast of the United States, 1960." *United States Fish and Wildlife Service, Special Scientific Report—Fisheries No. 550*. Washington, D.C., 1967. https://books.google.com/books.

Wayne, A.T. "Birds of South Carolina." Contributions from the Charleston Museum. Edited by P.M. Rea. 1910. https://archive.org/details/birdsofsouthcaro00wayn.

Weir, R.M. *Colonial South Carolina: A History*. Millwood, NY: KTO Press, 1983.

Wilson, S. "An Account of the Province of Carolina, by Samuel Wilson, 1682." In *Narratives of Early Carolina 1650–1708*. Edited by A.S. Salley Jr. New York: Charles Scribner's Sons, 1911.

Wood, P.H. *Black Majority: Negroes in Colonial South Carolina from 1670 through the Stono Rebellion*. New York: Alfred A. Knopf, 2012.

———. "'It Was a Negro Taught Them': A New Look at African Labor in Early South Carolina." In *Discovering Afro-America*. Edited by R.D. Abrahams and J.F. Szwed. Leiden, NL: E.J. Brill, 1975.

Wyche, B.W. "Tidelands and the Public Trust: An Application for South Carolina." *Ecology Law Quarterly* 7 (1978): 137–70. https://scholarship.law.berkeley.edu.

Index

About the Author

James O. Luken is associate dean and professor of biology at Coastal Carolina University. His research, generally focused on plant ecology and botany, has ranged from Alaska to Florida. Recent work with students and colleagues attempts to elucidate the mostly unknown natural history of the Venus flytrap and also seeks to quantify the cryptic natural capital of coastal ecosystems. He is a frequent consultant on managing working lands within the context of conservation easements. His publications include books, edited volumes and journal articles, as well as popular science articles on angling, travel and plants. Early mornings often find him on the waterways of Horry County in search of opportunities to catch fish.